W9-CLR-061

the

vintage

workshop®

Gifts

for All

Occasions

WITHDRAWN
No longer the property of the
Boston Public Library.
Sale of this material benefits the Library.

Baby Photos

the
vintage
workshop®
Gifts
for All
Occasions

Amy Barickman

Martingale®
& COMPANY

Credits

President: Nancy J. Martin
CEO: Daniel J. Martin
Publisher: Jane Hamada
Editorial Director: Mary V. Green
Managing Editor: Tina Cook
Technical Editor: Dawn Anderson
Copy Editor: Ellen Balstad
Design Director: Stan Green
Illustrator: Laurel Strand
Cover and Text Designer: Constance Bollen, cb graphics
Photographers: Bill Lindner Photography and Brent Kane

The Vintage Workshop: Gifts for All Occasions
© 2004 by Amy Barickman

Martingale & Company
20205 144th Avenue NE
Woodinville, WA 98072-8478 USA
www.martingale-pub.com

Printed in China
09 08 07 06 05 04   8 7 6 5 4 3 2 1

MISSION STATEMENT
Dedicated to providing quality products
and service to inspire creativity.

No part of this product may be reproduced in any form, unless otherwise stated, in which case reproduction is limited to the use of the purchaser. The written instructions, photographs, designs, projects, and patterns are intended for the personal, noncommercial use of the retail purchaser and are under federal copyright laws; they are not to be reproduced by any electronic, mechanical, or other means, including informational storage or retrieval systems, for commercial use. Permission is granted to photocopy patterns for the personal use of the retail purchaser.

The information in this book is presented in good faith, but no warranty is given nor results guaranteed. Since Martingale & Company has no control over choice of materials or procedures, the company assumes no responsibility for the use of this information.

Library of Congress Cataloging-in-Publication Data

Barickman, Amy.
    The Vintage Workshop : gifts for all occasions / Amy Barickman.
        p. cm.
    ISBN 1-56477-575-5
    1. Decalcomania. 2. Transfer-printing. 3. Iron-on transfers. 4. Gifts. 5. Handicraft. I. Title.
    TT880.B296 2004
    745.7—dc22
                                                                2004010491

DEDICATION

To my husband and business partner, Bob,
who has always been my strongest supporter through
the ups and downs of our careers,
a wonderful husband, and most importantly, an awesome father
to our precious children, Jack and Emma.
Your patience amazes me.

Acknowledgments

I would like to extend special thanks to all of those individuals who have contributed to the success of Indygo Junction and The Vintage Workshop. They have given their time and talents to our companies. They all have offered invaluable support, influenced me creatively, and amazed me with their talents. They are Vintage Workshop designers Michelle Spaw, Kathy Fernholz, and Natalie Acuff, who created the gorgeous projects featured in this book.

Other designers who are part of our workshop have inspired us and helped us grow our Click-n-Craft® business: Delsie Chambon, Desiree Mueller, Mary Ann Donze, Cathy Pendleton, Sarah Sporrer, Nanette Stewart, Greg Johnson, Carolyn Goodard, Sherry White, Tamara Vandergriff, Marge Wooters, Donna Gilbert, and Margaret Cox.

I also want to recognize the following people for their contributions: The Vintage Workshop's CD-ROM photographer Tracy Thompson; programming and digital designers Brooks Protzman, Brenda Tietze, Linda Cunningham, and Melinda Scrivner; and designer Amy Babcock.

And I want to give extra special thanks to the following people: Kayte Price, art director and designer; Jean Lowe, my agent; Polly Blair, content manager; Bridget Lowe, writer; Mary Green, editorial director of Martingale & Company; and Dawn Anderson, technical editor for this book.

Finally, my mother, Donna Martin, and my grandmother, Mildred Conrad, deserve special recognition for their creative inspiration through the years.

Contents

Cute as a Button: Crafts for Baby and Nursery — 19

Queen of the Castle: Crafts to Make the Home a Little More Homey — 39

The Dressy Desk: Crafts That Make Paying Bills More Fun — 55

Every Day Is a Holiday: Crafts to Celebrate the Holidays Throughout the Year — 73

The Welcome Mat: Crafts That Say "I Care" — 103

The Classy Classroom: Crafts for a Schoolroom with Style — 115

Introduction

~

Computer crafting has never been so easy or so accessible. *The Vintage Workshop: Gifts for All Occasions* features beautiful projects using old-fashioned images, and the companion Click-n-Craft CD-ROM contains all of these images so that you can print them with your home inkjet printer. In these pages, you'll find classic designs that employ crafting and needlework techniques ranging from beginner to advanced. There are delightful gifts for every occasion presented here.

The Vintage Workshop: Gifts for All Occasions combines the skills and talents of experienced designers, bringing you traditional looks and trendier styles, all in one complete collection.

We created these projects with a combination of readily available fabrics, papers, and trims to make these projects accessible to crafters everywhere. At the back of the book, you'll find a listing of many of the resources used so that you can achieve the exact look that we did. Or you can substitute our suggestions with your own unique style, combining vintage fabrics in your collection with old lace and buttons if that's your preference.

The ease with which images can be printed on various materials is truly amazing. With the accompanying Click-n-Craft CD-ROM, you can click on an image, print it out on a variety of papers and fabrics, and either sew, press, or transfer your image to a wealth of personalized gifts. Your gifts will become cherished treasures to all who receive them. So enjoy the experience! You can't go wrong if you have a computer and an inkjet printer. This collection promises to inspire the creative spirit within you.

Amy Barickman
Founder, The Vintage Workshop

The Click-n-Craft CD-ROM Art Collection

~

All of the images used for projects in this book are available on the Click-n-Craft CD-ROM packaged with this book. The images in the art collection have been scanned at a high resolution and sized for the projects in the book. Other vintage art featured throughout the book is available on other Click-n-Craft CDs or from downloadable art collections through the Vintage Workshop's Web site.

The opening screen that will appear
when you insert the Click-n-Craft CD-ROM.

Now from your own computer "workbench," one-of-a-kind, vintage-inspired designs are just a click away. When you meld the images from this vintage collection with modern inkjet-compatible products, you can create timeless gifts, wearables, decorative items, and memories. There is so much you can do!

Printing Instructions

To print the presized images found on the Click-n-Craft CD-ROM, simply click on the image for the project you are working on as it appears within the art collection. From the Adobe Acrobat Reader File Menu, choose Print, or click on the printer icon on the tool bar. Your image will print to size for each project. No adjustment or editing is required.

Editing Images

If you want to resize an image, you can edit any portable document format (pdf) image by using the Graphics Tool from Acrobat Reader 5.0 (included on the Click-n-Craft CD-ROM.). Put the crossbar on the top left corner of the image, and click and drag the editing box around the image. Right click and select Copy.

Next, minimize your screen and launch your word-processing program. In a new document, right click and paste the image into the new file. From there you may click on the image to move or resize it.

Gallery of Click-n-Craft
CD-ROM Images

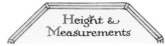

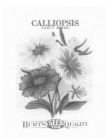

Guests

Project Supplies

The items described in this section and shown in the photo above may prove to be invaluable as you embark on making your vintage-inspired creations.

Inkjet-Compatible Products

Images can be printed on a variety of inkjet-compatible products, including papers, fabric sheets, iron-on transfer sheets, labels, vellum sheets, and magnet sheets. Most of these products are straightforward—just print and you're done! However, make sure that you always read the product instructions before you begin. Also note that inkjet fabric sheets need a little extra attention, as we will explain.

Most inkjet fabric sheets have a paper backing to help feed them through a printer. Be sure to trim any loose strings or fibers from the fabric sheets before placing them in the printer. Also determine which side to run face-up in your printer before you print the image. It's always a good idea to test-run the image on plain paper first. Once you print the image on the fabric, simply peel off the paper backing to release the fabric.

Many inkjet fabrics are colorfast. We haven't encountered any difficulties, but just to be sure it's best to hand wash or dry-clean your finished fabric projects. For extra durability, colorfastness, and waterproofing, you might elect to spray your image with a clear acrylic coating, such as Krylon No. 1303.

Materials

A variety of different materials are used to create the projects in this book. Each project has a list of the materials needed. Some projects start with a ready-made item such as an apron, journal, picture frame, or baby blanket, and are embellished with vintage images and trims. Other projects are made from scratch, allowing you even more options for personalizing them. Either way you will be able to incorporate an endless array of products such as fabrics, scraps of ribbon or trim, fibers, embroidery floss, decorative papers, assorted buttons, and acrylic craft paint. For embellishing, consider both old and new decorative objects to reinvent and re-create the projects.

Adhesives

You will use an assortment of adhesives for the projects, including glue sticks, fabric or craft glue, hot-glue guns, spray-mounting adhesives, fusible tapes, and paper-backed iron-on adhesives for fabric appliqués. Follow the manufacturer's recommendations for compatibility of adhesives with various materials and surfaces. When using spray adhesives, be sure to protect your work surface with kraft paper or newspaper.

Tools

Each project in the book has a list of tools needed. The tools vary with each project. For sewing projects, you will need general sewing supplies such as a sewing machine, a rotary cutter and cutting mat, scissors, pins, needles, an iron, and an ironing board. For painting projects, you will need items such as

Inkjet Media from The Vintage Workshop

The Vintage Workshop is your source for inkjet materials. Visit our Web site to see our complete collection of printable fabrics, papers, and transfers. Information on how to reach us can be found in the "Resource Directory" on page 126. Note that the performance of our inkjet products can be affected by humidity and storage conditions. For best results, store the inkjet products flat in low-humidity conditions. The Vintage Workshop inkjet fabric, in addition to being stored flat, should also be placed in a bag or between two pieces of cardboard. The fabric can be touched without fear of leaving fingerprints or removing the finish.

For best results, feed only one product sheet at a time into the printer. Make sure your inkjet product is facing the right way (face up or face down) in your printer—always test on a regular sheet of paper first. We prefer images that are printed on a matte-finish paper. There are many varieties on the market to choose from. Adhesive label sheets can be substituted for paper. We also frequently use an inkjet vellum sheet. Don't be afraid to experiment with different options.

sandpaper and foam brushes. For paper projects, it is helpful to have a craft knife and cutting mat, and a metal ruler with a cork back. You may also want to use some specialty tools such as a hole punch, decorative paper edgers, or an eyelet setting tool to install eyelets.

Vintage Looks with Modern Flair

Scratch the "made from scratch"—time is precious! Embellish purchased, ready-made objects and garments with your favorite vintage images!

❶

Start with something new:

- ❧ Computer image software
- ❧ Inkjet-compatible products
- ❧ Creative edging tools
- ❧ Decorative paper
- ❧ Colored paper eyelets

❷

Add something with a vintage look:

- ❧ Vintage images from the Click-n-Craft CD-ROM at the back of this book, to link the present with the past
- ❧ Hand stitching
- ❧ Buttons
- ❧ Old-fashioned fabrics
- ❧ Fibers such as ribbons and threads

❸

And end up with something wonderful!

Creating with vintage art is fun, fast, and easy. Start by printing a beautiful piece of art from the Click-n-Craft CD-ROM onto the surface of your choice, and then make it special simply by using a pair of decorative paper edgers. Cut it out and voilà! You have a beautiful tag or card instantly ready to tie

onto a package that you're taking to a shower or a holiday party. Or quick-print an image and apply it to the front of an ordinary journal. Keep a few supplies on hand so that you can make quick, personal hostess gifts, baby gifts, birthday gifts, and more. It's so easy but it means so much to people to receive something made by hand.

When you make a gift, it becomes a keepsake forever. The little touches that go into the details make an everyday sentiment extra-special. The Vintage Workshop designers provide all of the basic instructions you need to make the projects that appear in this book. We also provide inspiration for you to think about the possibilities of making gifts for

Embellishing Ideas

- Use eyelets—alone or clustered—for dimension.

- Weave ribbon through eyelets and tie ends.

- Set an eyelet at each opening edge on the front and back of a card or journal and tie a ribbon through the holes for a finishing accent.

- Add a frame of vellum with a center cut from corner to corner in an X shape over a vintage image. Roll the center vellum back to reveal the image underneath.

- Use a large needle to punch evenly spaced holes around the perimeter of a card and hand stitch a decorative edge with embroidery floss or linen thread.

- Layer the background behind an image with fabric or decorative paper for dimension and charm.

- Consider tearing edges of paper randomly instead of trimming them straight.

- Add a single or double paper mat around an image or photo, allowing for at least a $\frac{1}{16}$" border all around to make the image stand out.

- Don't forget the pages inside of a journal. This is a great place to add little vintage images.

- Secure photos, vintage images, or vellum overlays to a piece of paper with small metal eyelets in the corners or along the top of the piece.

- For journals, attach simple phrases or quotes to each page for a more artistic touch. Handwrite or print words on a vellum sheet, trim to size, and adhere to the page.

- Print vintage art or photos directly onto vellum or a Vintage Workshop Click-n-Craft Gloss Finish Artist Canvas Sheet for a special look.

others or personalizing your home decor. The Vintage Workshop has more than 16 CD-ROM art collections that are currently available in craft stores and fabric stores, as well as on our Web site www.thevintageworkshop.com. Crafting has never been so easy! Modern technology allows crafters everywhere to use their home computer systems to create beautiful gifts. Visit our Web site for more ideas and projects, inspiration, the latest news in computer crafting, downloadable art, and current technical updates.

Whether you're dressing up your home with handmade embellishments or giving your creations as gifts, you'll find all the information you need in this book to get started with this exciting new way of using modern technology. The Vintage Workshop would like you to consider us your source for information, images, projects, and inspiration. This book is a wonderful opportunity for us to share our style with you. We welcome your input as well, so please visit us online.

Baby Photos

Crafts for Baby and Nursery

Cute as a Button

*Every baby born into the world
is a finer one than the last.*

—Charles Dickens

The anticipated arrival of a new baby is one of the most exciting times in life, and preparing a cheerful space for the baby is part of the fun. The projects in this chapter will not only delight the recipient—they are also easy enough to finish in plenty of time for the baby shower.

This bounty of keepsakes for a baby's nursery will be cherished for years to come. Start with a cozy pillow and blanket, personalized with your choice of images. Offer parents-to-be the gift of handcrafted birth announcements. Or, give a coordinating growth chart and journal set to highlight the baby's first years.

With these design ideas—and your own original touches—the baby's room will be cute as a button, just like the baby!

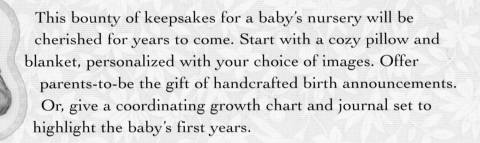

*What does little baby weigh
Laughing, merry, full of play?
To his mother I am told,
He is worth his weight in gold.*

—Traditional verse

Materials

**1 Vintage Workshop
Click-n-Craft Cotton
Poplin Fabric Sheet**

∾

**1 strip of fabric,
2" x 38",
for pillow front flange**

∾

**1 square of fabric,
11" x 11",
for the pillow back**

∾

Polyester fiberfill

∾

Thread to match fabric

∾

**Clear monofilament
thread**

Tools

Clear grid ruler

∾

Hand-sewing needle

∾

Iron and ironing board

∾

Pins

∾

**Rotary cutter and
cutting mat**

∾

Scissors

∾

Scrap fabric

∾

Sewing machine

Sleeping Baby Pillow

Cutting dimensions include ¼" seam allowances.

❶ From the Click-n-Craft CD-ROM, print the sleeping baby pillow image onto the inkjet fabric sheet, following the manufacturer's instructions.

❷ Trim the image to 8" square. Remove the paper backing from the image.

❸ From the fabric strip for the pillow front flange, cut two strips 2" x 8" and two strips 2" x 11" long. With right sides together, pin a 2" x 8" fabric strip along the right side of the image, matching raw edges. Stitch. Repeat on the left side of the image to make a unit as shown in figure 1. Press seams toward the strips.

❹ With right sides together, pin a 2" x 11" fabric strip along the top of the image, matching raw edges. Stitch. Repeat along the bottom of the image to make a unit a shown in figure 2. Press seams toward the strips.

Fig. 1

❺ With right sides together, pin the pillow front to the pillow back. Stitch around all sides, leaving a 3" opening along the bottom for turning. Clip corners, turn right side out, and press.

❻ Replace the upper thread in your sewing machine with the monofilament thread. To prevent thread breakage, you

Fig. 2

may have to lessen the tension depending upon your machine. Test on scrap fabric before stitching on your pillow.

❼ Stitch in the ditch around the image, leaving a 3" opening along the bottom of the image for stuffing. (To "stitch in the

ditch" means that you stitch right on the seam line so that the stitching is hidden in the seam.)

8 Stuff the pillow with polyester fiberfill.

9 Stitch in the ditch along the opening at the bottom of the image.

10 Slip-stitch the opening closed along the outer edge of the pillow.

Materials

Wire-bound journal,
horizontal format, 8" x 6"*

∾

1 sheet of high-quality
inkjet paper, matte finish

∾

1 sheet of decorative
paper, such as
scrapbook paper

∾

Spray Mount
Artist's Adhesive

∾

Colored eyelets to fit holes
along wire binding
(optional)

*So that you can easily remove
and replace the cover, choose a journal bound with wire loops that you
can pull apart rather than
one bound with a single
spiral of wire.*

Tools

Craft knife and
cutting mat

∾

Eyelet setting tool and
hammer (optional, to
install eyelets)

∾

Hole punch to
match size of holes
along wire binding

∾

Metal ruler
with cork back

1 Remove the front cover from the wire binding. For best results, pull the wire binding apart slightly where the ends meet.

2 Lay the cover flat on your work surface. With Spray Mount, adhere the decorative paper to the front of the journal cover. Apply slight pressure to secure it in place. Trim away the excess paper with a craft knife.

3 With a hole punch, punch through the decorative paper covering the holes. If desired, install eyelets at each hole, following the manufacturer's instructions.

4 From the Click-n-Craft CD-ROM, print the baby photo album image onto the inkjet paper. Cut out the image. With Spray Mount, adhere the image to the center of the cover, applying slight pressure to secure it in place.

5 Reattach the cover to the journal. For best results, align the cover holes to the wire binding where the ends meet. Gently reposition it into place. Press the wire sections together to close the gap where the ends of the binding meet.

Tip
To make this project even easier, purchase a journal that already has a solid or patterned cover that coordinates with the baby photo album image.

**1 Vintage Workshop
Click-n-Craft Cotton
Poplin Fabric Sheet**

❧

**Purchased or handmade
baby blanket**

❧

**Ribbon, about ⅜" wide
(amount determined in
step 1 of "Assembly for
Baby Blanket")**

❧

Thread to match ribbon

❧

**4 buttons, about ⅜"
in diameter (optional)***

❧

**4" x 6" piece of
paper-backed iron-on
adhesive**

❧

Fusible tape, ¼"-wide

**If you expect the blanket
to be used heavily (rather than
decoratively), omit the buttons to
eliminate a choking hazard.*

Tools
for Baby Blanket

Clear grid ruler

❧

Hand-sewing needle

❧

Iron and ironing board

❧

**Rotary cutter and
cutting mat**

❧

Scissors

❧

Sewing machine

❧

Tape measure

Sleeping Baby Blanket
and Hanger Cover

Assembly for Baby Blanket

❶ To determine the ribbon yardage for edging the sides of the blanket, measure around the sides of the blanket about 5" in from the outer edge and record the measurement. To this measurement, add about 26" for bordering the image and turning under the raw edges at the ends. If desired, you can add bows at the four corners of the blanket as well. Add 60" more to make four bows.

❷ From the Click-n-Craft CD-ROM, print the sleeping baby blanket image onto the inkjet fabric sheet, following the manufacturer's instructions.

❸ Trim the image to include a ¼" border on all sides. Remove the paper backing from the image.

❹ Fuse the image to the paper-backed iron-on adhesive, following the manufacturer's instructions.

❺ Determine the location for the image. Consider putting it in a corner, along one side of the blanket, or in the center of the blanket. Remove the paper backing from the iron-on adhesive and fuse the image in place, following the manufacturer's instructions. The image on the blanket on page 25 was placed diagonally in a corner, about 10½" in from the outer edge of the fringe at the corner.

❻ Cut two pieces of ribbon the same length as the long side of the image. Following the manufacturer's instructions, use fusible tape to secure the ribbon to the long edges of the image over the ¼" border. Cut two pieces of ribbon the same length as the short side of the image, plus ½". Press under ¼" on each end. Use fusible tape to secure the ribbon to the short edges of the image. Machine stitch along both edges of the ribbon all around.

7 Apply ribbon to the four sides of the blanket, 5" in from the outer edge, as in step 6. Add bows to the corners of the blanket, if desired. To add bows, cut a 15" length of ribbon and tie it into a bow. Hand stitch the bow securely to one corner of the blanket. Repeat at the remaining corners.

8 If desired, stitch buttons securely to the corners of the image over the ribbon.

▶ ▶ ▶

Materials for Hanger Cover

1 Vintage Workshop Click-n-Craft Cotton Poplin Fabric Sheet

∞

¼ yard of outer fabric for cover

∞

¼ yard of coordinating fabric for lining and binding

∞

¼ yard of fusible interfacing

∞

4" x 4" piece of paper-backed iron-on adhesive

∞

Fusible tape, ¼"-wide, or hand-sewing needle

∞

Thread to match fabrics

∞

Hanger for child-size clothing

Tools for Hanger Cover

Clear grid ruler

∞

Iron and ironing board

∞

Paper for pattern

∞

Pencil

∞

Pins

∞

Rotary cutter and cutting mat

∞

Scissors

∞

Sewing machine

Assembly for Hanger Cover

Cutting dimensions include ¼" seam allowances.

❶ To make the pattern, place the hanger on a piece of paper. Trace around the top, omitting the hook, and around the curve on each side and stop. Remove the hanger. Measure down 1½" from the points where you stopped on each side and make a mark. Draw a horizontal line to connect the two marks as shown in figure 1. Next, make a vertical line on each side that connects the bottom of the curve to the horizontal line. Add ¼" all around your pattern for the seam allowance as shown in figure 2. Cut the pattern out of the paper.

❷ With the pattern, cut two pieces from the outer fabric, two from the lining fabric, and two from the fusible interfacing.

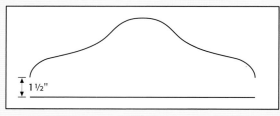

Fig. 1

❸ Fuse the interfacing to the wrong side of each lining piece.

❹ Match each outer fabric piece with a lining piece, wrong sides together. Baste around the edges of each unit.

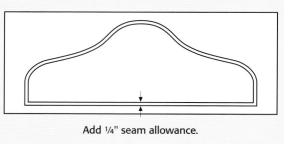

Add ¼" seam allowance.

Fig. 2

❺ With outer fabrics facing, pin the two hanger units together. Stitch around the top and sides, leaving about a ⅜" opening at the center top where the hanger wire will go.

❻ Turn the cover right side out. Put the cover on the hanger and see if you like how it fits. If not, make adjustments. When you are satisfied, trim the seams, turn right side out and press.

❼ Secure the seam allowances in place around the opening at the top of the cover by hand sewing or fusing with tape, following the manufacturer's instructions.

❽ To make the binding for the lower edge of the cover, cut a 1½"-wide strip of binding fabric the length needed to go around

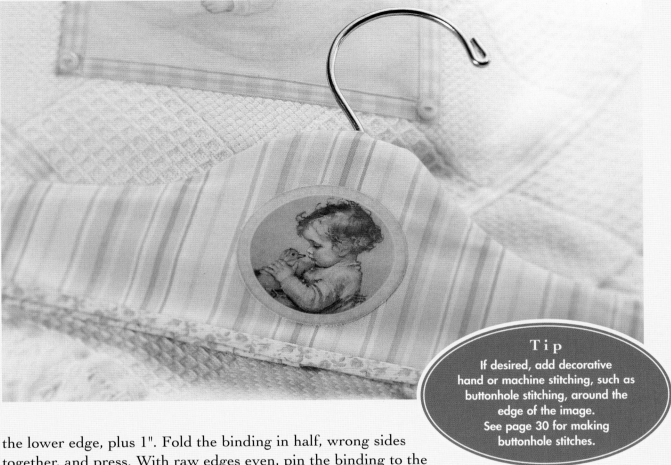

Tip
If desired, add decorative
hand or machine stitching, such as
buttonhole stitching, around the
edge of the image.
See page 30 for making
buttonhole stitches.

the lower edge, plus 1". Fold the binding in half, wrong sides together, and press. With raw edges even, pin the binding to the right side of the cover, being sure to tuck the binding ends under where they meet. Fold the binding to the inside and slip-stitch in place by hand or secure with fusible tape, following the manufacturer's instructions.

9 From the Click-n-Craft CD-ROM, print the hanger cover image (there are four per page) onto the inkjet fabric sheet, following the manufacturer's instructions. Trim an image to include a ½" border on all sides.

10 Remove the paper backing from the image. Fuse the image to the fusible interfacing, following the manufacturer's instructions. Then fuse the image to a piece of iron-on adhesive, following the manufacturer's instructions. Cut out the image.

11 Remove the paper backing from the iron-on adhesive. Center the image on the front side of the hanger cover and fuse in place, following the manufacturer's instructions.

12 Insert hanger into cover.

Materials

1 sheet of high-quality inkjet paper, matte finish*

∾

Metal pail, about 6" tall x 6" diameter at top

∾

Blue enamel spray paint

∾

Aerosol primer for metal surfaces

∾

1 sheet of decorative patterned paper, such as scrapbook paper

∾

Spray Mount Artist's Adhesive

* If you want your image to be removable, consider printing the image directly to a magnet sheet. This would eliminate the need for the patterned-paper border.

Tools

Craft knife and cutting mat

∾

Metal ruler with cork back

∾

Newspaper

∾

Painter's tape

Baby Pail

1 Cover the work surface with newspaper. Apply painter's tape to the inside of the pail around the upper edge. Line the inside of the pail with newspaper to protect it from spray paint and primer.

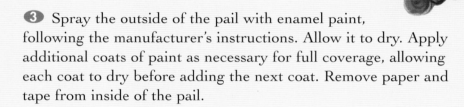

2 Spray the outside of the pail with primer, following the manufacturer's instructions. Allow it to dry. Apply a second coat of primer and allow it to dry.

3 Spray the outside of the pail with enamel paint, following the manufacturer's instructions. Allow it to dry. Apply additional coats of paint as necessary for full coverage, allowing each coat to dry before adding the next coat. Remove paper and tape from inside of the pail.

4 From the Click-n-Craft CD-ROM, print the baby pail image onto inkjet paper. Cut out the image.

5 With Spray Mount, adhere the image to the sheet of patterned paper, applying slight pressure to secure it in place. Trim the patterned paper ¼" from the edges of the image, leaving a narrow border around the image.

6 With Spray Mount, adhere the image to the front of the pail, applying slight pressure to secure it in place.

Materials

3 Vintage Workshop
Click-n-Craft Cotton
Canvas Fabric Sheets

❧

Purchased fabric growth
chart, about 10" x 41"*

❧

2 buttons, about ⅜"
in diameter

❧

Thread or embroidery
floss to match
growth chart

❧

Contrasting thread
for buttons

❧

10" x 15" piece of
paper-backed iron-on
adhesive

*We found ours at BagWorks
(www.bagworks.com).*

Tools

Clear grid ruler

❧

Embroidery needle
(optional, for decorative
hand stitching)

❧

Hand-sewing needle

❧

Iron and ironing board

❧

Rotary cutter and
cutting mat

❧

Scissors

❧

Sewing machine
(optional, for decorative
machine stitching)

Growth Chart

1 From the Click-n-Craft CD-ROM, print the five growth chart images and the height and measurements image onto the fabric sheets. For best results, print the images with only one sheet in the printer at a time.

2 Cut each image out, leaving a ½" border around all the edges. Remove the paper backing from the images.

3 Fuse each image to the paper-backed iron-on adhesive, following the manufacturer's instructions. Trim the images to their exact sizes. For the height and measurements image, trim around the image along the top and sides and then ¼" below the word *measurements* along the bottom.

4 Center the height and measurements image across the top of the growth chart and arrange the remaining five images evenly down the left side. Remove the paper backing from the images and fuse in place, following the manufacturer's instructions.

5 Stitch around the edges of the images with a decorative machine stitch, such as a buttonhole stitch, or stitch around the images with two strands of embroidery floss and a hand-buttonhole stitch as shown at right.

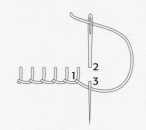

Buttonhole Stitch

6 With contrasting thread, sew a button to each side of the height and measurements image along the lower edge, referring to the photo for placement.

Materials

**1 Vintage Workshop
Click-n-Craft Iron-On
Transfer II Sheet**

∾

**Purchased tank top for
infant or toddler**

∾

**Thread or embroidery
floss to match image**

Tools

Clear grid ruler

∾

**Embroidery needle
(optional, for decorative
hand stitching)**

∾

Iron and ironing board

∾

Pins

∾

Pressing cloth

∾

**Rotary cutter and
cutting mat**

∾

Scissors

∾

**Sewing machine
(optional, for decorative
machine stitching)**

Baby Rose Tank Top

① From the Click-n-Craft CD-ROM, print the baby rose tank top image (there are two per page) onto the inkjet transfer sheet, following the manufacturer's instructions. Cut out an image.

② Pin-mark the vertical center of the tank top. Center the image 1" down from the top edge of the tank top. Remove the pins. Use a pressing cloth and follow the manufacturer's instructions to fuse the image onto the tank top.

③ Stitch around the edges of the image with a decorative machine stitch, such as a buttonhole stitch, or stitch around the image with two strands of embroidery floss and a hand-buttonhole stitch (see page 30 for making buttonhole stitches by hand).

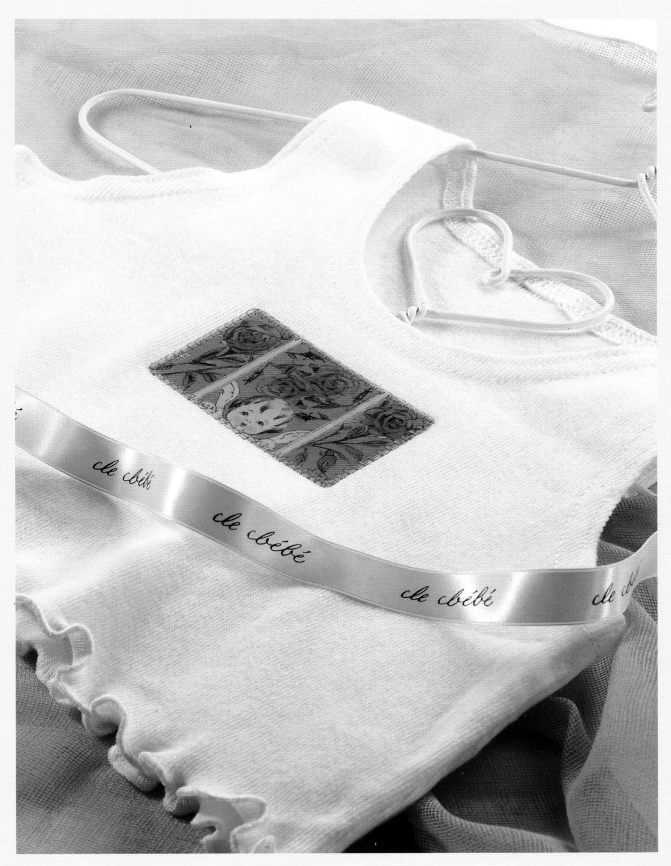

Materials

1 sheet of high-quality inkjet paper, matte finish

∾

Single or double switch plate (wood or plastic)

∾

Lightweight patterned paper, such as scrapbook paper, wrapping paper, or tissue paper

∾

Craft glue

∾

Glue stick

Tools

Craft knife and cutting mat

∾

Foam brush

Nursery Switch Plates

1 With a foam brush, apply craft glue to the front surface of the switch plate. Adhere patterned paper to the front of the switch plate, rubbing firmly to eliminate any air bubbles. Trim excess paper around the edges and center opening(s) with a craft knife.

2 From the Click-n-Craft CD-ROM, print the nursery switch plate images onto inkjet paper. Use a small image for a single switch plate or a large image for a double switch plate. Trim around the images with a craft knife.

3 With a glue stick, adhere the images to the surface of the switch plate, applying slight pressure to secure in place. Refer to the photo for placement.

**2 Vintage Workshop
Click-n-Craft Gloss Finish
Artist Canvas Sheets**

**6 sheets of coordinating
card stock**

**¼ yard of cotton
background fabric**

**⅛ yard of coordinating
cotton fabric for border**

Embroidery floss

**Spray Mount
Artist's Adhesive**

Fray Check

Craft glue

Tools

**Cork-backed
metal ruler**

**Craft knife and
cutting mat**

Embroidery needle

Pinking shears

Scissors

Just Flown In
Baby Announcement

❶ From the Click-n-Craft CD-ROM, print the baby announcement image onto the inkjet canvas sheets (three images to a sheet). Cut out the images.

❷ For each card, cut a 5¼" square from the card stock and a 5¾" square from the background fabric.

❸ Apply Spray Mount to the wrong side of the square of background fabric, center the fabric over one side of the card stock square, and press in place. Wrap the excess fabric to the back side, securing with craft glue at the corners, if necessary.

❹ Apply Spray Mount to the wrong side of a canvas image and adhere it to the border fabric. Apply Fray Check to the border fabric ⅜" out from the edges of the image, and allow it to dry.

❺ Cut ⅜" from the edges of the image with pinking shears to create a border. With embroidery floss and tack stitches, stitch around the edges of the image. Place stitches about ⅜" apart.

❻ With craft glue, adhere the bordered image to the upper portion of the fabric-covered square of card stock. Leave the edges unglued for more dimension.

❼ With a computer and a word processing program, design the layout of the name and monogram (we used the Typo Upright font for the Lucy June Dunne card and the Copperplate Gothic Heavy font for the Wiley Birch Acuff card). Duplicate the monogram for use on the back of the envelope. Print both the name label and envelope monogram onto coordinating card stock. With a craft knife, cut out a 1⅛" x 4¾" rectangle from the card stock for the name label, centering the name and monogram within the rectangle. Adhere the name label to the bottom of the announcement with Spray Mount. Set aside the envelope monogram.

❽ Cut a 5⅛" square of card stock and adhere it to the back of the card with Spray Mount. Note that this piece could be printed with additional information or could be left blank for a handwritten personal greeting.

9 To personalize the envelope, cut out the envelope monogram you created in step 7 and adhere it to a scrap of background fabric or border fabric with Spray Mount. Apply Fray Check to the fabric ⅜" from the edges of the monogram rectangle and allow it to dry. Cut ⅜" from the edges of the monogram rectangle with pinking shears. Adhere the monogram with its new border to the back of the envelope flap with Spray Mount.

Crafts to Make the Home a Little More Homey

Queen of the Castle

I remember, I remember
The house where I was born,
The little window where the sun
Came peeping in at morn.

— Thomas Hood

Personal touches are what make a house a home. This chapter is filled with easy projects that can quickly transform a so-so space into something special. From charming votive candles and keepsake boxes to pamper-me projects that are perfect for gifts and holiday presents, you'll find designs to make your home sparkle.

Delightful seed-packet artwork is perfect for adorning garden totes and hats. They'll make great gifts for your gardening friends! You'll also discover how easy it is to create beautiful stationery with your home computer, and how to embellish a "sew cute" pillow to dress up your living spaces.

Look to this chapter again and again for inspiring gift ideas for friends and family. But don't forget to treat yourself to these keepsakes! The time spent creating one of these lovely decorative items is its own reward.

'Mid pleasures and palaces though we may roam,
Be it ever so humble, there's no place like home.

— John Howard Payne

Materials

1 Vintage Workshop
Click-n-Craft Cotton
Canvas Fabric Sheet

Canvas or straw tote

¼ yard of fabric
for border

10" x 15" piece of
paper-backed iron-on
adhesive

Tools

Clear grid ruler

Iron and ironing board

Rotary cutter and
cutting mat

Scissors

❶ From the Click-n-Craft
CD-ROM, print the seed packet tote image
on the cotton canvas inkjet fabric sheet.
Cut out the image, which includes a
¼" border on all sides. Press the
¼" border to the back of the image
on all sides.

❷ Fuse a piece of paper-backed
iron-on adhesive, cut to fit, to the
wrong side of the image, following the
manufacturer's instructions. Set it aside.

❸ Cut a 7" x 9½" rectangle from the fabric.
Turn ¼" to the wrong side along the edges and
press. Fuse a piece of paper-backed iron-on
adhesive, cut to fit, to the wrong side of the
rectangle, following the manufacturer's instructions.

❹ Remove the paper backing from the fabric rectangle and
fuse the rectangle to the center front of the tote as desired,
following the manufacturer's instructions. Remove the paper
backing from the seed packet image. Center and fuse the seed
packet image to the front of the fabric rectangle, also following
the manufacturer's instructions.

Materials

1 Vintage Workshop
Click-n-Craft Cotton
Canvas Fabric Sheet

Canvas or straw hat

¼ yard of fabric
for hatband

4 buttons, ½"-wide

Thread to match fabric
and canvas sheet

Contrasting embroidery
floss for buttons

Fusible tape, ¼"-wide

Tools

Clear grid ruler

Embroidery needle

Hand-sewing needle

Iron and ironing board

Rotary cutter and
cutting mat

Scissors

Sewing machine

Seed Packet Hat

Cutting dimensions include ¼" seam allowances.

❶ From the Click-n-Craft CD-ROM, print the three seed packet hat images onto the cotton canvas inkjet fabric sheet. Cut out the images, each of which includes a ¼" border on all sides. Press the border to the back of each image on all sides. Set the images aside.

❷ Measure the circumference around the hat where the band will be placed and add ½" for overlap. Cut a 2¾"-wide fabric strip to the measured length. Also cut a 2¾" x 15" strip for the bow and a 2¾" x 3" strip for the center wrap around the bow. With right sides together, fold each strip in half lengthwise and stitch along the long raw edges. Turn each piece right side out, center the seam on one side, and press.

❸ Apply fusible tape to the hatband along the seam line, following the manufacturer's instructions. Remove the paper backing from the tape and fuse the band to the hat, following the manufacturer's instructions. Overlap the edges at the center back.

❹ Fold in the ends of the 15" strip to the center, seam side in, overlapping the ends. Tack in place. Wrap the 3" strip around the center join, overlapping the ends, and tack in place. Stitch the bow to the center back of the hat over the hatband ends.

❺ Hand tack the seed packet images, centered over the band front and spaced about 1" apart as shown in the photo.

❻ Use floss to sew the buttons to the band as shown. Tie a knot on the top of each button and trim the ends ¼" from the knots.

Keepsake Box

Materials

1 Vintage Workshop Click-n-Craft Gloss Finish Artist Canvas Sheet

✦

Unfinished wood box, 5¼" wide x 8" long x 3" high

✦

Acrylic gesso primer

✦

Green acrylic craft paint

✦

Yellow acrylic craft paint

✦

Spray Mount Artist's Adhesive

Tools

Craft knife and cutting mat

✦

Foam brush

✦

Metal ruler with cork back

✦

Sandpaper, fine-grit

❶ With the foam brush, cover the entire surface of the wood box with acrylic primer. Allow to dry. Apply a second coat of primer and allow to dry. Sand the box lightly with fine-grit sandpaper.

❷ With the foam brush, cover the surface of the box with green acrylic craft paint. Allow to dry. With a clean foam brush, cover the surface of the box with yellow acrylic craft paint. Allow to dry. Apply a second coat of yellow paint if necessary for good coverage. Allow to dry.

❸ Sand the box lightly with sandpaper, especially along the edges to reveal the layers of green paint and white gesso.

❹ From the Click-n-Craft CD-ROM, print the keepsake box image onto the inkjet artist canvas sheet. Cut out the image.

❺ With Spray Mount, adhere the image to the lid of the box, applying slight pressure to secure it in place.

Materials for 9 Magnets

3 Vintage Workshop Click-n-Craft Magnet Sheets

2 or more sheets of card stock in desired colors for borders

Spray Mount Artist's Adhesive

Tools

Craft knife and cutting mat

Metal ruler with cork back

❶ From the Click-n-Craft CD-ROM, print the magnet images onto one of the inkjet magnet sheets, following the manufacturer's instructions. Cut out the images, just inside the marked lines.

❷ Cut nine 3" x 4" rectangles from the desired card stock. With Spray Mount, adhere the rectangles to the remaining inkjet magnet sheets.

❸ Using Spray Mount, adhere the rose images to the rectangles of card stock, centering the roses. Trim about ⅛" from the edges of the rose images to create borders.

Materials
for 15 Sheets of
Stationery or
15 Greeting Cards

1 sheet of high-quality inkjet paper, matte finish

∞

15 sheets of heavyweight paper, such as card stock, for stationery, or 8 sheets of 12" x 12" card stock for greeting cards

∞

2 sheets of lightweight patterned paper, such as scrapbook paper

∞

Spray Mount Artist's Adhesive

Tools

Craft knife and cutting mat

∞

Metal ruler with cork back

∞

Pinking paper edgers

Personalized Stationery

❶ From the Click-n-Craft CD-ROM, print the flower images onto the inkjet paper. Trim the images just inside the marked lines.

❷ With Spray Mount, adhere the images to the lightweight patterned paper, allowing at least ⅜" between the images. Apply slight pressure to secure the images in place.

❸ Trim along the edges of the images with pinking paper edgers to create a pinked border.

❹ For the greeting cards, cut two 4½" x 6" rectangles from each piece of card stock. Fold each rectangle in half to create a card that measures 4½" x 3".

❺ For the greeting cards, use Spray Mount to adhere the images to the left side of the card fronts, applying slight pressure to secure them in place. For the stationery, use Spray Mount to adhere each image to the upper left-hand corner of a piece of heavyweight paper.

Tip
To quickly create a set of greeting cards, start with a set of plain white blank greeting cards and matching envelopes and simply adhere the stationery images to the upper left corner of the cards or to the center front of the cards.

Materials for 3 Candles

3 pillar candles—
3¾" x 6", 3" x 9",
and 2¾" x 4"

❧

1 Vintage Workshop
Click-n-Craft
Vellum Sheet with
adhesive backing

Tools

Craft knife and
cutting mat

❧

Metal ruler with
cork back

Rose Pillar Candles

CAUTION: *Candles should be large enough to burn from center and not from circumference. Labels should never be close to flame or hot wax. Never leave burning candles unattended.*

❶ From the Click-n-Craft CD-ROM, print the rose candle images onto the clear, full-sheet inkjet label, following the manufacturer's instructions. Cut out the images.

❷ Peel back the top left corner of the paper backing on one image and gently lift the backing from the left edge of the label. Position the label on the desired candle, smoothing the left edge down. Continue to remove the paper backing with one hand while smoothing the label in place. This will keep air bubbles from forming under the label. Repeat for the remaining candles.

Materials

1 Vintage Workshop
Click-n-Craft Cotton
Poplin Fabric Sheet

∾

2 squares of cotton fabric,
each 10½" x 10½"

∾

1¼ yards of fringe trim,
1¼" long

∾

9" x 9" piece of
paper-backed iron-on
adhesive

∾

Polyester fiberfill

∾

Thread to match fabric
and trim

∾

Thread or embroidery
floss for decorative
stitching around image

Tools

Clear grid ruler

∾

Embroidery needle
(for decorative
hand-stitching, optional)

∾

Hand-sewing needle

∾

Iron and ironing board

∾

Pins

∾

Rotary cutter and
cutting mat

∾

Scissors

∾

Sewing machine

Sew Cute Pillow

Cutting dimensions include ¼" seam allowances.

1 From the Click-n-Craft CD-ROM, print the pillow image onto the inkjet fabric sheet, following the manufacturer's instructions. Trim the image ¼" from the outer edges.

2 Remove the paper backing from the image. Fuse the image to the paper-backed iron-on adhesive, following the manufacturer's instructions. Cut the image out exactly around the edges.

3 Remove the paper backing from the image. Center the image on a 10½" square of fabric, and fuse it in place following the manufacturer's instructions.

4 Stitch around the edges of the image with a decorative machine stitch, such as a buttonhole stitch, or stitch around the image with two strands of embroidery floss and a hand-buttonhole stitch (see page 30 for making buttonhole stitches by hand).

5 With right sides together, pin the pillow front square to the pillow back square. Stitch around the edges, leaving a 4" opening on one side for turning. Turn the pillow right side out and press.

6 Stuff the pillow with polyester fiberfill. Slip-stitch the opening closed.

7 Pin the fringe trim to the outer edges of the pillow, keeping the edge of the trim even with the outer edge of the pillow. Hand stitch in place.

Crafts that Make Paying Bills More Fun
The Dressy Desk

*My desk, most loyal friend
thank you. You've been with me on
every road I've taken.*

— Marina Tsvetaeva

Is the space you've made for taking care of household business a comfortable place to spend time? If your home desk is a mess of bills, letters, and sticky notes, the projects in this section will help you organize your workspace effectively—and give it a good dash of style.

Creating a relaxed setting for correspondence begins with chic storage. In this chapter you'll find a pencil box with classic flair and an expandable file that doubles as art, plus a clever way to organize those scattered CDs. Add your own personal touches with a mail holder, a tissue box adorned with vintage art, and an eye-catching glass paperweight.

Whether you are sitting down to pay the monthly bills, drawing up a weekly menu, or writing a letter to a faraway friend, rely on these fast, fun projects to customize your desk and transform it into a spot where you want to linger.

*Sir, more than kisses, letters mingle souls;
For, thus friends absent speak.*

— John Donne

Materials for Expandable File

1 sheet of high-quality inkjet paper, matte finish

∞

Expandable (accordion) office file, horizontal format, 9½" x 4½"

∞

1 sheet of solid card stock, 12" x 12"

∞

1 sheet of script paper, such as scrapbook paper, 12" x 12"

∞

1 sheet of striped paper, such as scrapbook paper, 12" x 12"

∞

Spray Mount Artist's Adhesive

∞

Velcro dots (with adhesive back) for closure

Tools for Expandable File

Bone folder or table knife

∞

Craft knife and cutting mat

∞

Metal ruler with cork back

∞

Scissors

Assembly for Expandable File

1 If your expandable file has a flap closure that wraps over the front of the file, remove it by trimming it off along the upper back edge of the file. Measure the front, top, and back of the expandable file and cut a piece of solid card stock to this size to wrap around it. With Spray Mount, adhere the paper to the back of the file, aligning the edges. Score the paper along the upper back edge of the file and then along the upper front edge by dragging a bone folder or dull edge of a table knife along the edge of the ruler. Fold the paper along the scored lines so that it wraps around to the front of the file, creating a front flap. Trim off a I" strip of the solid paper along the lower edge of the front flap. See figure 1.

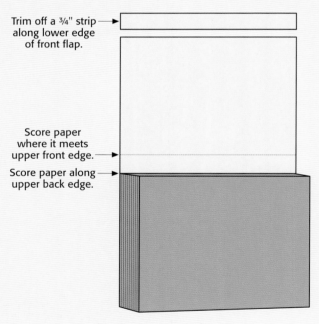

Trim off a ¾" strip along lower edge of front flap.

Score paper where it meets upper front edge.

Score paper along upper back edge.

Fig. 1

2 Measure the file front and cut one piece of striped paper to the exact dimensions and cut a second piece of paper ⅜" larger on the two short sides and on one long side. Also cut a strip of striped paper that measures 2" by the width of the file. Cut the striped paper so that the stripes run vertically on each piece.

▶ ▶ ▶

❸ With Spray Mount, adhere the 2"-wide strip of paper, wrong sides together and edges aligned along one long side, to the striped paper cut to the exact dimensions of the file front. With Spray Mount, adhere this piece, 2"-wide strip facing out, to the back side of the solid front flap of the file. This will create a ¾" striped border along the lower edge of the front flap and line the inside of the flap with striped paper as shown in figure 2.

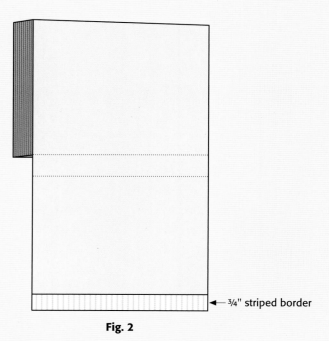

← ¾" striped border

Fig. 2

❹ With Spray Mount, adhere the remaining piece of striped paper to the front of the file, under the flap, aligning the top edges. Fold the side and bottom edges around the file between the accordion folds, trimming away excess paper at the lower corners as necessary.

❺ Measure the front flap and cut a piece of script paper to those dimensions. Trim 1" from one long edge. Using Spray Mount, adhere the script paper to the front flap, aligning the top and side edges and leaving a ¼" solid border and a ¾" striped border along the lower edge of the flap.

❻ From the Click-n-Craft CD-ROM, print the flower image onto inkjet paper. Cut out the image.

7 With Spray Mount, adhere the image to the center of the front of flap, applying slight pressure to secure it in place.

8 Attach the loop side of the Velcro dot to the inside of the flap at the center of the lower edge. Attach the hook side of the Velcro dot under the flap at the corresponding point along the lower edge of the file front.

~

Assembly for Glass Paperweight

1 Lay paperweight on top of lightweight piece of board. With a pencil, trace around the outer edge of the paperweight. Cut just inside the pencil lines with a craft knife. This becomes the background surface for the paper collage.

2 Cut or tear the decorative papers into desired shapes and sizes. With Spray Mount, adhere the decorative papers as desired to the background surface, creating a collage. Trim off any excess paper around the edge of the background board with a craft knife.

3 From the Click-n-Craft CD-ROM, print the cat onto inkjet paper. Trim close to the edge of the cat image. Glue the cat image to the center of the background board.

4 With a word processing program, create a label with the name of the cat, if desired. Select a font and point size of your choice. Print the name onto solid paper, and then cut out the printed name. To create a border around the name, glue the name to a piece of decorative paper and cut or tear the decorative paper 1/8" from the edge of the solid paper to create the label. Glue the label to the background board, just below the cat image, to finish the collage.

5 Place a small amount of glass adhesive around the outer edge of the background board on the front side. Align the paperweight on top of the board, centering the collage, and press firmly to secure it together. Allow it to dry overnight.

Materials for Glass Paperweight

1 sheet of high-quality inkjet paper, matte finish

Glass paperweight, 3½" diameter

4" x 4" piece of lightweight board, such as mat board

Scraps of decorative paper, such as scrapbook paper and vintage postage stamps, in green, rose, tan, and ivory

Spray Mount Artist's Adhesive

Adhesive designed for use on glass, such as E-6000

Tools for Glass Paperweight

Craft knife and cutting mat

Metal ruler with cork back

Pencil

Materials

1 sheet of high-quality inkjet paper, matte finish

✿

Wood cigar box, 10¼" x 6½"

✿

Lightweight paper, such as patterned gift tissue paper or scrapbook paper (about 3 sheets)

✿

2 different sheets of coordinating solid-color scrapbook paper or card stock

✿

Spray Mount Artist's Adhesive

✿

Craft glue

Tools

Craft knife and cutting mat

✿

Foam brush

✿

Metal ruler with cork back

❶ With a foam brush, apply a thin coat of craft glue to the lid of the box. Lay the lightweight paper over the surface of the lid and smooth out the paper with your fingers to eliminate any wrinkles. Trim away the excess paper with a craft knife. Repeat the process for the sides of the box until the surface is completely covered.

❷ From the Click-n-Craft CD-ROM, print the pencil box image onto inkjet paper. Be sure to pretest the printing on scrap paper first to check for accurate orientation of the image and adjust as necessary. Cut out the image.

❸ With Spray Mount, adhere the image to a sheet of solid paper, applying slight pressure to secure in place. Trim ¹⁄₁₆" from the edges of the image on all sides to create a narrow border.

❹ With Spray Mount, adhere the image to a second sheet of coordinating solid paper. Apply slight pressure to secure in place. Trim ⅛" from the edges of the first border to create a second narrow border.

❺ With Spray Mount, adhere the image to the center front of the box lid. Apply slight pressure to secure it in place.

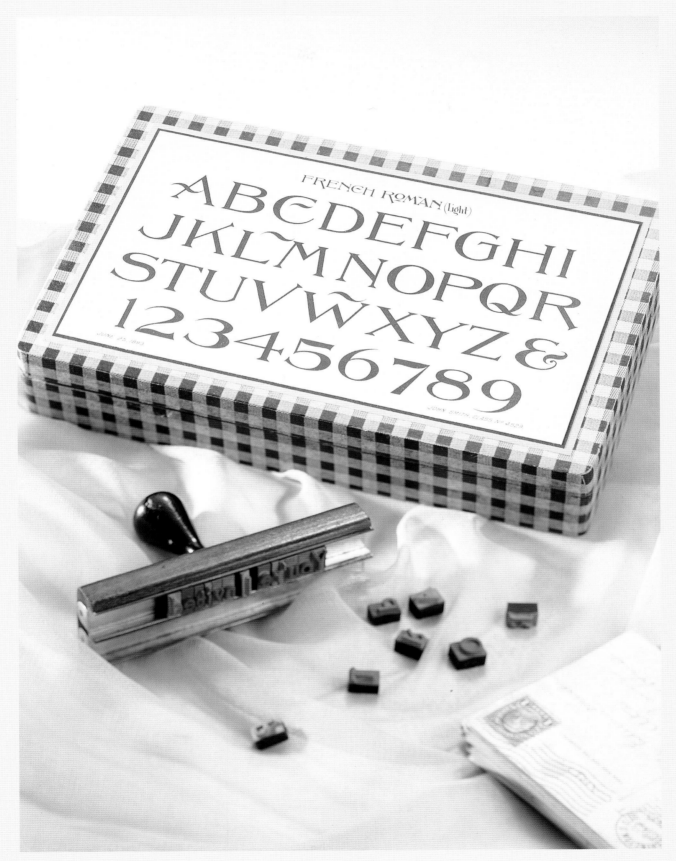

Materials

1 sheet of high-quality inkjet paper, matte finish

∾

Tissue box (painted wood or plastic, about 6" wide x 6" long x 6½" high)

∾

1 sheet of card stock

∾

Spray Mount Artist's Adhesive

Tools

Craft knife and cutting mat

∾

Metal ruler with cork back

Tissue Box

❶ From the Click-n-Craft CD-ROM, print the tissue box image onto inkjet paper. Cut out the image.

❷ With Spray Mount, adhere the image to a piece of card stock. Cut ⅛" from the edge of the image to create a narrow border.

❸ With Spray Mount, adhere the image to the front of the tissue box, applying slight pressure to secure it in place.

Materials for 3 Boxes

1 sheet of high-quality inkjet paper, matte finish

∾

3 ivory papier-mâché boxes, 3⅛" wide x 4¼" long x 2½" high

∾

1 sheet of striped paper, such as scrapbook paper

∾

Spray Mount Artist's Adhesive

Tools

Craft knife and cutting mat

∾

Metal ruler with cork back

❶ From the Click-n-Craft CD-ROM, print the three office box images onto inkjet paper. Cut out the images.

❷ With Spray Mount, adhere the images to the striped paper, allowing at least ½" between the images and applying slight pressure to secure them in place. Trim ³⁄₁₆" from the side edges of each image to create narrow side borders. Trim paper even with the top and bottom of each image.

❸ With Spray Mount, adhere the images to the box lids, applying slight pressure to secure them in place.

Materials

1 Vintage Workshop
Click-n-Craft Iron-On
Transfer II Sheet

∾

¾ yard of fabric

∾

1 package (4 yards) of
¼"-wide, double-fold,
black bias tape

∾

1 package (3 yards) of
½"-wide, folded,
black bias tape

∾

2 pieces of fusible
interfacing, 11" x 22"

∾

¼"-wide fusible tape

Tools

Clear grid ruler

∾

Iron and ironing board

∾

Pins

∾

Rotary cutter and
cutting mat

∾

Scissors

∾

Sewing machine

Hanging Mail Holder

Cutting dimensions include ¼" seam allowances.

❶ From the Click-n-Craft CD-ROM, print the five hanging mail holder images onto the iron-on inkjet transfer sheet, following the manufacturer's instructions. Cut out the images and set aside.

❷ From the fabric, cut two 11" x 22" rectangles for the front and back of the mail holder. Also cut two 11" x 4⅞" rectangles for the top two pockets and one 11" x 4⅝" rectangle for the bottom pocket.

❸ Finish the long raw edges of the three pocket sections with a zigzag stitch. Fold ¼" to the wrong side along one long edge of the 11" x 4⅞" rectangles. This will be the lower edge.

❹ Press one 11" x 4⅞" pocket section in half crosswise. Center the image "Pens" between one edge and the pressed center. Center the image "Misc" between the other edge and the pressed center. Fuse the images in place, following the manufacturer's instructions.

❺ Center the "Mail" image on the remaining 11" x 4⅞" pocket section and center the "Bills" image on the final pocket section. Fuse in place, following the manufacturer's instructions.

❻ Apply the ¼"-wide bias tape to the upper edge of each pocket section, following the manufacturer's instructions. Set the pocket sections aside.

❼ Fuse the interfacing pieces to the wrong sides of the 11" x 22" fabric rectangles. Center the postcard image on the right side of

▶ ▶ ▶

one of the rectangles 1½" down from the upper edge. Fuse in place, following the manufacturer's instructions.

8 With wrong sides together, baste the front and back 11" x 22" rectangles together a scant ¼" from the raw edges.

9 Pin the top edge of the "Mail" pocket 6¼" down from the upper edge. Edgestitch along the bottom edge of the pocket, next to the fold. Baste along the side edges as shown in figure 1.

10 Pin the bottom "Bills" pocket along the bottom of the mail holder, aligning the lower and side edges. Baste in place as shown in figure 2.

11 Center the "Pens & Misc" pocket in between the top and bottom pockets. Edgestitch along the bottom edge of the pocket,

Someone, somewhere, wants a letter from you.

—**British Post Office slogan**

Fig. 1

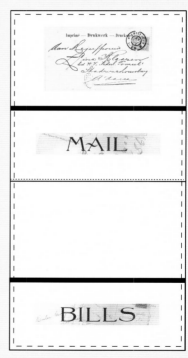

Fig. 2

next to the fold. Baste along the side edges. Stitch a vertical line at the center of the pocket to divide the pocket in half evenly as shown in figure 3.

⓬ Apply the ½"-wide bias tape to the long side edges of the mail holder, following the manufacturer's instructions. Trim the bias tape even with the top and bottom edges of the mail holder. Apply bias tape to the top and bottom edges of the mail holder, turning under ¼" at each end.

⓭ Cut two 4" pieces of ¼"-wide bias tape. Open up the bias tape and insert a piece of fusible tape between the fold. Refold the bias tape and fuse with the iron to seal the strip closed. Fold each strip in half to make a loop. Attach the loops to the upper edge of the mail holder 2½" from the side edges with a small piece of fusible tape.

Fig. 3

1 sheet of high-quality,
matte-finish inkjet paper

∽

2 sheets of 12" x 12"
heavyweight paper,
such as card stock

∽

Glue stick

∽

Spray Mount
Artist's Adhesive

∽

¾ yard of cording,
about ⅛" diameter

Tools

⅛" hole punch

∽

Bone folder or table knife

∽

Craft knife and
cutting mat

∽

Metal ruler with
cork back

∽

Pencil

CD Holder

1 Cut each sheet of card stock to 5¾" x 11". Measure in ¼" along the long edges and mark a line with a pencil. Score along the pencil lines to form a crease. For best results, lay a ruler against the pencil lines and run a bone folder or the dull edge of a table knife along the edge of the ruler. Fold in the paper along the scored lines. Score the paper again 5½" from one short edge. Fold along the scored line to create a 5¼" x 5½" envelope.

2 With a glue stick, place adhesive along the side tabs and press together to form an envelope.

3 From the Click-n-Craft CD-ROM, print the CD holder images onto inkjet paper. Cut out the two images. With Spray Mount, adhere each image to the front of an envelope, aligning it with the glued side edges and the folded edge. Apply slight pressure to secure it in place.

4 Punch a small hole at the top center of each envelope, through both layers of paper. Cut the cording into two equal lengths. For each envelope, insert cording through both holes and knot the ends to create a tie closure.

> **Tip**
> To make this project even easier, print the CD holder image onto a sheet of Vintage Workshop Click-n-Craft matte paper with adhesive backing. The adhesive backing on the paper eliminates the need for using Spray Mount.

Crafts to Celebrate the Holidays Throughout the Year

Every Day Is a Holiday

The most wasted of all days is that on which one has not laughed.

—Nicolas Chamfort

Establishing holiday traditions for your family—whether it's a hearty meal, a summertime picnic, or an annual sing-along—is what creates memories for generations to come. Bringing out festive items to display in the home is another wonderful way to inspire the holiday spirit in everyone around you.

Of course, sharing gifts with friends and loved ones is another popular way to jump-start the holidays, and in this chapter you'll find ideas for Valentine's Day, Mother's Day, Independence Day, Halloween, and Christmas. Projects with a touch of old-fashioned whimsy include greeting cards, totes, a banner, a pillow, and even a sweet candy box.

So make time for a little handcrafted fun during the holidays! Browse these pages and you'll see how easy it is to bring your own handmade touch to celebrating in style.

We are the music-makers,
and we are the dreamers of dreams.

—Arthur William Edgar O'Shaughnessy

73

Materials for 3 Valentine Cards

1 sheet of high-quality inkjet paper, matte finish

Decorative paper such as scrapbook paper
(1 sheet each of solid red and red striped)

1 sheet each of white, medium pink, and light pink card stock

¼ yard of ribbon for pink rose heart card

¼ yard of narrow cording, ⅛" in diameter, for "With My Love" tag

Spray Mount Artist's Adhesive

Craft glue

Tools for 3 Valentine Cards

⅛" hole punch

Bone folder or table knife

Craft knife and cutting mat

Metal ruler with cork back

Pinking paper edgers and scalloped paper edgers

Assembly for Valentine Cards

❶ From the Click-n-Craft CD-ROM, print the valentine images onto inkjet paper. With the scalloped paper edgers, trim the With My Love image into a rectangle measuring approximately 2¾" x 1¾". Trim around the edges of the rose heart with a craft knife, cutting away the extra background. Trim the Valentine Greetings and To My Valentine images along the edges. Set the images aside.

❷ **Pink rose heart card:** Cut a 3¼" x 7" rectangle from the white card stock. Score the paper crosswise in the center by dragging a bone folder or the dull edge of a table knife along the edge of a ruler. Fold on the scored line to make a 3¼" x 3½" card. Cut a piece of solid red paper to cover just a little more than the upper one-third of the card. Cut a piece of red striped paper to cover the lower portion of the card. Adhere the papers in place with Spray Mount. Also use Spray Mount to adhere the rose heart valentine image to the center of the card front, applying slight pressure to secure it in place. Tie ribbon in a bow and trim the tails at an angle. Glue the bow to the bottom of the rose heart image.

>>>

74

To My Valentine card: Adhere the To My Valentine image to a piece of medium pink card stock with Spray Mount. Trim around the image with the pinking paper edgers to create a narrow pinked border. Adhere the image to a piece of light pink card stock and trim ¼" beyond the edges of the image to create a narrow pink border. Cut a piece of medium pink card stock 5" x 7". Score the paper crosswise in the center by dragging a bone folder or the dull edge of a table knife along the edge of a ruler. Fold on the scored line to make a 5" x 3½" card. Trim around the three cut edges of the card with the pinking paper edgers to create a narrow pinked border. With Spray Mount, adhere the bordered image to the front of the card.

With My Love tag: Cut a 3⅜" x 2" rectangle of solid red paper. With Spray Mount, adhere the With My Love image to the center of the rectangle. With Spray Mount, adhere the bordered image to a piece of light pink card stock. Trim ⅛" from the edges of the red paper to create a narrow light pink border. Punch a hole in the upper left corner of the tag. Thread the cording through the hole and knot the ends together.

**1 sheet of high-quality
inkjet paper, matte finish**

**1 sheet of card stock,
12" x 12", for box**

**⅜ yard of narrow
cording, ⅛" diameter**

Glue stick

**Spray Mount
Artist's Adhesive**

**Decorative tissue,
candy, or small toys
to fill the box**

*Tools for Valentine
Candy Box*

⅛" hole punch

Bone folder or table knife

**Craft knife and
cutting mat**

**Metal ruler with
cork back**

Pencil with eraser

Assembly for
Valentine Candy Box

❶ Photocopy the pattern on page 79, enlarging it by 125%. Cut out the pattern. Place the pattern on the card stock and trace around it. Cut on the marked lines.

❷ Score along the dashed fold lines by running a bone folder or the dull edge of a table knife along the edge of a ruler. Fold the paper along the scored lines.

❸ With Spray Mount, adhere the valentine image to the outside of section F on the card stock, applying slight pressure to secure it in place.

➤ ➤ ➤

4 Apply glue stick to the inside of flap G. Fold the box along the fold lines with the image on the outside and adhere flap G over flap C. Press firmly to secure. Allow it to dry for about five minutes.

5 Fold up flaps H and J and apply glue stick to the outside edges. Tuck the flaps to the inside of the box. Press flap J firmly against the bottom of section D, and then press flap H firmly against section I. Set the box on a hard surface and insert the eraser end of a pencil into the box to tap flap H firmly against section I. Allow it to dry for about five minutes.

6 Punch a hole on the sides of the box as indicated on sections E and G of the pattern. Insert cording through the holes of the box from the outside and tie knots at the ends. Add decorative tissue to the inside of the box and fill with candy, small toys, or special mementos.

7 Fold flap A down and tuck into inside of box to form the lid.

Valentine Candy Box Pattern

Enlarge pattern 125%.

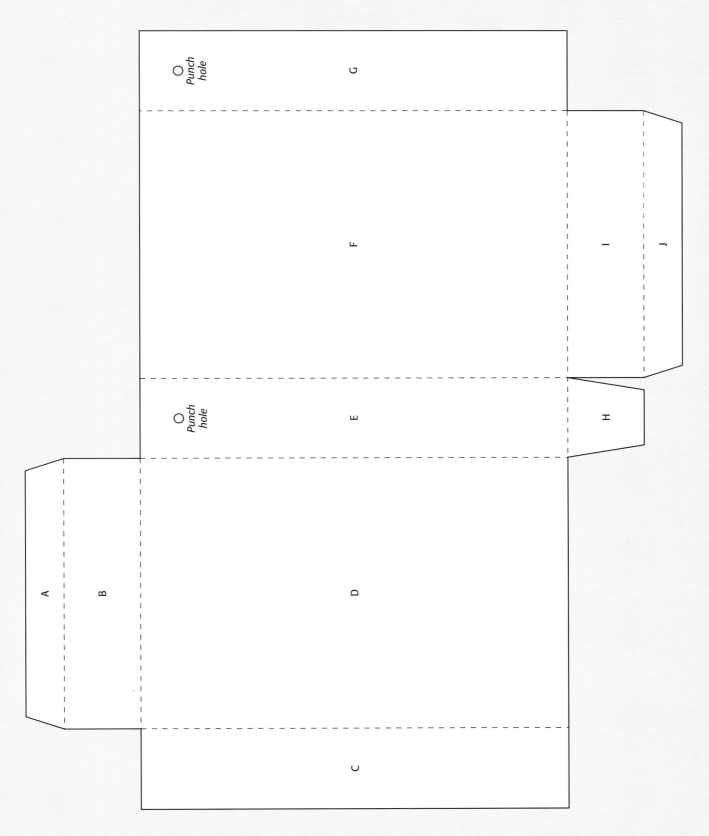

Mother's Day Cards

Materials for 2 Cards

1 Vintage Workshop
Click-n-Craft Gloss Finish
Artist Canvas Sheet

∾

Solid card stock
(1 sheet each of white, red,
pink, and pale blue)

∾

Spray Mount
Artist's Adhesive

∾

White or black photo
corners (4 per card)

Tools

Craft knife and
cutting mat

∾

Metal ruler with
cork back

∾

Bone folder
or table knife

❶ From the Click-n-Craft CD-ROM, print the two Mother's Day card images onto the inkjet artist canvas, following the manufacturer's instructions. Trim the mother and child image along the edges. Trim the image of the children ⅛" beyond the edges.

❷ For the mother and child card, use Spray Mount to adhere the image to a piece of red card stock, adding photo corners to the corners of the image. Trim the card stock ⅛" from the edges of the image. From the white card stock, cut a 3⅞" x 7⅞" piece. Score the paper crosswise in the center by dragging a bone folder or the dull edge of a table knife along the edge of a ruler. Fold on the scored line to make a 3⅞" x 3¹⁵⁄₁₆" card. Adhere the bordered image to the center front of the card with Spray Mount.

For the card with the children, use Spray Mount to adhere the image to a piece of pale blue card stock, adding photo corners to the corners of the image. Trim the card stock ⅛" from the edges of the image. From the pink card stock, cut an 11" x 4" piece. Score the paper crosswise in the center by dragging a bone folder or the dull edge of a table knife along the edge of a ruler. Fold on the scored line to make a 5½" x 4" card. Adhere the bordered image to the center front of the card with Spray Mount.

Materials

Materials

1 sheet of high-quality
inkjet paper, matte finish

∽

Wood frame for a 4" x 6"
photo (must have a smooth
surface, about 1⅝" wide)

∽

1 sheet of white card stock

∽

Glue stick

Tools

Tools

Craft knife and
cutting mat

∽

Metal ruler with
cork back

∽

Pinking paper edgers

Mother's Day Frame

❶ From the Click-n-Craft
CD-ROM, print the four Mother's
Day frame images onto inkjet
paper. Trim the images just outside
the outer border line.

❷ With a glue stick, adhere the
images to a piece of card stock,
allowing at least ½" between the
images and applying slight
pressure to secure them in place.
Cut around the images with
pinking paper edgers to create a
narrow pinked border around
each image.

❸ With a glue stick, adhere the images with the birds to the top
and bottom of the frame, centering the images and applying
slight pressure to secure them in place. Adhere the images
without birds to the sides of the frame.
Allow the project to dry thoroughly.

Tip
You can adjust the images
slightly for narrower frames. To make
the images smaller all around, simply
leave off the pinked borders. To make the
images slightly shorter in length, trim
off the flower enclosed in the
box at each end of
the image.

82

3 sheets of high-quality inkjet paper, matte finish

1 sheet of solid paper, such as card stock

Unfinished wood tray, about 11½" x 14½"

Acrylic gesso primer

Dark blue acrylic craft paint

Lightweight board, such as mat board, cut to the inside dimensions of the tray

Spray Mount Artist's Adhesive

Glue stick

Glass, cut to the inside dimensions of the tray

Tools

Craft knife and cutting mat

Foam brush

Metal ruler with cork back

Sandpaper, medium-grit

Liberty Tray

1 With gesso and a foam brush, prime the entire surface of the tray. Allow the tray to dry thoroughly. Apply a second coat of gesso and allow it to dry. With the foam brush, cover the surface of the tray with blue acrylic craft paint. Allow it to dry thoroughly as well.

2 Sand the surface of the tray lightly with medium-grit sandpaper, rubbing away part of the surface paint to create a distressed appearance.

3 From the Click-n-Craft CD-ROM, print the signature sheet onto two sheets of inkjet paper. Additional sheets may be necessary, depending on the size of the tray you select. Cut signature sheets into small shapes with straight or angled sides. With a glue stick, adhere the small pieces randomly around the outer 2" of the lightweight board. Overlap the pieces to create a collage effect for the background. Trim away any excess paper from the outer edges of the board with a craft knife.

4 From the Click-n-Craft CD-ROM, print the image of the woman onto inkjet paper. Cut out the image. With Spray Mount, adhere the image to a sheet of solid paper, applying slight pressure to secure it in place. Trim ¼" from the edges of the image to create a narrow border all around.

5 With Spray Mount, adhere the image to the center of the board, applying slight pressure to secure it in place. Place the board against the bottom of the tray, pressing firmly.

6 Place a piece of glass inside the bottom of the tray, covering the mat board.

Tip

Several sizes of precut glass are available from hobby and craft stores. If your tray is not a standard size, ask the frame department at your hobby or craft store to cut a piece of glass to fit.

Materials

1 Vintage Workshop
Click-n-Craft Cotton
Poplin Fabric Sheet

∞

¼ yard of yellow plaid
fabric for inner border
and tabs

∞

¼ yard of orange plaid
fabric for outer border

∞

16" x 19½" piece of fabric
for backing

∞

16" x 19½" piece of fusible
interfacing

∞

16" x 19½" piece of
cotton batting

∞

Thread to match fabrics

∞

Clear monofilament thread

∞

⅝" wood dowel rod,
18" long

∞

2 wood end caps for
dowel rod

∞

Wood stain

∞

Wood glue

Tools

Clear grid ruler

∞

Iron and ironing board

∞

Pins

∞

Rotary cutter and
cutting mat

∞

Scissors

∞

Sewing machine

86

Halloween Banner

Cutting dimensions include ¼" seam allowances.

❶ From the Click-n-Craft CD-ROM, print the Halloween banner image on the inkjet fabric sheet, following the manufacturer's instructions. Trim the image so that it has a ¼" border on all sides.

❷ From the yellow fabric, cut two strips 2" x 10½" and two strips 2" x 10" for the inner border. Also cut three strips 3" x 4½" for the tabs. From the orange fabric, cut two strips 3½" x 13½" and two strips 3½" x 16" for the outer border. Set the strips aside.

❸ With right sides together, pin one 2" x 10½" yellow fabric strip along the right side of the image, matching raw edges. Stitch. Repeat on the left side to make a unit as shown in figure 1. Press seam allowances toward the strips.

❹ With right sides together, pin a 2" x 10" yellow fabric strip along the top of the image, matching raw edges. Stitch. Repeat on the bottom of the image to make a unit as shown in figure 2. Press seam allowances toward the strips.

Fig. 1

Fig. 2

▶ ▶ ▶

Trick or Treat
Be so sweet
Give me something
Good to eat!

5 Stitch the orange outer-border strips to the banner in the same manner as the yellow inner-border strips. Stitch the 3½" x 13½" long strips to the sides first, and then stitch the 3½" x 16" strips to the top and bottom edges of the banner to make a unit as shown in figure 3. Press the seam allowances toward the strips.

6 With right sides together, fold the yellow strips for the tabs in half lengthwise and stitch along the long edges. Turn each strip right side out. Center the seam in the middle of one side and press.

7 Fold each strip in half, with the seam on the inside. Press.

8 Pin-mark the center of the banner along the top edge. Pin one tab at the center mark, matching raw edges. Pin the remaining tabs ⅜" in from the top corners. Baste tabs in place as shown in figure 4.

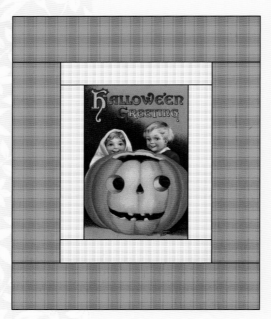

Fig. 3

Baste tabs in place.

Fig. 4

9 Fuse the interfacing to the wrong side of the banner backing piece. Baste the cotton batting to the back of the banner front.

10 Pin the banner front, batting side up, to the right side of the banner backing. Trim the banner backing, if necessary, so that it is exactly the same size as the banner front.

11 Stitch around all sides, leaving a 4" opening on one side for turning. Be careful not to catch the two corner tabs in the stitching.

12 Trim the corners. Turn the banner right side out and press. Slipstitch the opening closed.

13 Replace the upper thread in your sewing machine with the monofilament thread.

14 To secure the layers together, stitch in the ditch between the image and the borders. ("Stitch in the ditch" means that you stitch right on the seam line so that the stitching is hidden in the seam.) You may have to lessen the tension, depending upon your machine, to prevent the monofilament from breaking. Test on scrap fabric before stitching on your banner.

15 Stain the wood dowel rod and end caps, following the manufacturer's instructions. Let them dry completely.

16 Insert the dowel rod through the tabs and glue the end caps to the rod with wood glue. Allow the glue to dry.

Materials

1 Vintage Workshop
Click-n-Craft Cotton
Poplin Fabric Sheet

∾

⅜ yard of fabric for outer
bag and handles

∾

⅛ yard of fabric
for front band

∾

⅜ yard of fabric for lining

∾

¾ yard of fusible interfacing

∾

⅜ yard of ribbon trim,
¼" wide

∾

4" x 6" piece of paper-
backed iron-on adhesive

∾

Fusible tape, ¼" wide

∾

Thread to match fabrics

∾

Contrasting thread or
embroidery floss for
decorative stitching

Tools

Clear grid ruler

∾

Embroidery needle
(optional, for decorative
hand stitching)

∾

Hand-sewing needle

∾

Iron and ironing board

∾

Pins

∾

Pencil

∾

Rotary cutter and
cutting mat

∾

Scissors

∾

Sewing machine

Halloween Tote

Cutting dimensions include ¼" seam allowances.

❶ From the outer bag fabric, cut two 12" x 14" rectangles for the outer bag and two 3" x 10½" rectangles for the handles. From the lining fabric, cut two 12" x 14" rectangles. From the front band fabric, cut one 12" x 4" rectangle. From the fusible interfacing, cut two 12" x 14" rectangles for the bag and two 3" x 10½" rectangles for the handles.

❷ Fuse the interfacing rectangles to the wrong sides of the outer bag rectangles, following the manufacturer's instructions.

❸ On one long edge of the band piece, turn under ¼" and press. Position the band, right side up, on the right side of one of the outer bag rectangles, aligning the raw edges along the upper and side edges. Pin in place. Stitch along the edge of the fold and use longer basting stitches around the remaining three sides as shown in figure 1.

❹ With fusible tape, fuse the ribbon trim over the seam line between the outer bag and the band, following the manufac- turer's instructions. Trim off the excess trim.

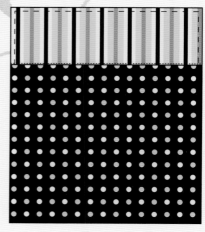

Stitch front band in place.

Fig. 1

❺ From the Click-n-Craft CD-ROM, print the Halloween tote image onto the inkjet fabric sheet, following the manufacturer's instruc- tions. Trim the image so that it has a ¼" border on all sides. Remove the paper backing from the image. Press the ¼" borders to the back of the image on all sides.

❻ Fuse the image to the piece of paper-backed iron-on adhesive, following the manufacturer's instructions. Remove the paper backing.

> > >

7 Center the image on the front of the bag, 1" below the trim. Fuse it in place, following the manufacturer's instructions.

8 Stitch around the edges of the image with a decorative machine stitch, such as a buttonhole stitch, or stitch around the image with two strands of embroidery floss and a hand-buttonhole stitch (see page 30 for making buttonhole stitches by hand).

9 Pin the bag front to the back, right sides together. Stitch around the side and bottom edges. Press the seams open.

10 With right sides together, pinch the side seam down to meet the bottom seam, lining them up, one on top of another. Secure with a pin. Measure in 1½" from the corner point and draw a line. Stitch on this line as shown in figure 2. Trim ¼" away from this stitching. Repeat for the other corner. Set the bag aside.

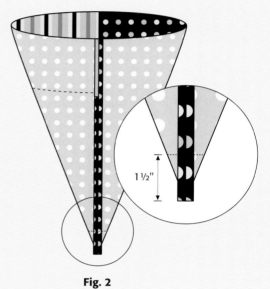

Fig. 2

11 Pin the lining pieces right sides together. Stitch around the sides and bottom, leaving a 4" opening along the bottom for turning. Follow step 10 for the lining, and then set the lining aside.

12 Fuse the handle interfacing pieces to the wrong sides of the handle pieces, following the manufacturer's instructions.

13 With right sides together, fold each strap piece in half lengthwise and stitch along the long edges. Turn the handles right side out, centering the seam down the middle of the strap, and press.

14 Pin-mark the center of the bag front and back along the upper edge. Measure 1" to each side of the center mark and pin-mark. With right sides together, align the handles with the upper edge of the bag just to the outside of the pin marks and baste in place as shown in figure 3.

15 Turn the bag right side out. Insert the bag into the lining, right sides together, and pin around the upper edge. Stitch around the upper edge. Turn the bag right side out through the opening in the lining. Insert the lining into the bag. Press along the upper edge.

16 Slip-stitch the opening in the lining closed.

Baste handles in place.

Fig. 3

T i p
To help the bag hold its shape at the bottom, cut a piece of plastic canvas to measure 3" x 8½" and insert into the bottom of the bag.

Materials

1 Vintage Workshop
Click-n-Craft Cotton
Poplin Fabric Sheet

Purchased tote bag,
about 9" x 13½"

5" x 8" piece of
paper-backed iron-on
fusible adhesive

Thread for decorative
machine stitching or
embroidery floss for
decorative hand stitching

Tools

Clear grid ruler

Iron and ironing board

Rotary cutter and
cutting mat

Scissors

Sewing machine for
decorative machine
stitching or embroidery
needle for decorative
hand stitching

Hearty Christmas Greetings

❶ From the Click-n-Craft CD-ROM, print the Christmas tote image onto the inkjet fabric sheet, following the manufacturer's instructions. Trim the image so that it has a ¼" border on all sides. Remove the paper backing from the image.

❷ Press the ¼" borders to the back of the image on all sides.

❸ Fuse the image to the piece of paper-backed iron-on adhesive, following the manufacturer's instructions. Remove the paper backing.

❹ Center the image on the front of the bag. Fuse it in place, following the manufacturer's instructions.

❺ Stitch around the edges of the image with a decorative machine stitch, such as a buttonhole stitch, or stitch around the image with two strands of embroidery floss and a hand-buttonhole stitch (see page 30 for making buttonhole stitches by hand).

Materials

**1 Vintage Workshop
Click-n-Craft Cotton
Poplin Fabric Sheet**

~

**2 pieces of fabric,
each 8½" x 10½", for the
pillow front and back**

~

**2 pieces of fusible
interfacing,
each 8½" x 10½"**

~

1¼ yards of fringe trim

~

¾ yard of braid trim

~

**4½" x 6¼" piece of paper-
backed iron-on adhesive**

~

Polyester fiberfill

~

**4 buttons, about ⅝"
in diameter**

~

**Thread to match fabric
and trim**

~

**Contrasting thread
for buttons**

Tools

Clear grid ruler

~

Hand-sewing needle

~

Iron and ironing board

~

Pins

~

**Rotary cutter and
cutting mat**

~

Scissors

~

Sewing machine

Christmas Pillow

Cutting dimensions include ¼" seam allowances.

❶ From the Click-n-Craft
CD-ROM, print the
Christmas pillow image onto
the inkjet fabric sheet,
following the manufacturer's
instructions. Trim the image
so that it has a ¼" border on
all sides. Remove the paper
backing from the image.

❷ Press the ¼" borders to
the back of the image on all
sides.

❸ Fuse the image to the piece of paper-backed iron-on
adhesive, following the manufacturer's instructions. Remove the
paper backing.

❹ Center the image on the right side of one of the 8½" x 10½"
fabric rectangles and fuse in place, following the manufacturer's
instructions.

❺ Fuse the interfacing rectangles to the wrong sides of the
8½" x 10½" fabric rectangles, following the manufacturer's
instructions.

❻ Stitch braid trim around the outer edges of the image,
stitching along both edges of the trim. With contrasting thread,
sew a button to each corner of the image over the braid trim.

❼ Pin the pillow front to the pillow back, right sides together.
Stitch around all edges, leaving a 4" opening at the bottom for
turning.

❽ Clip corners, turn right side out, and press.

❾ Pin the fringe trim to the pillow cover, ½" from the raw
edges and starting at the bottom opening. Machine stitch along

the inner edge of the fringe trim, leaving a 4" opening along the bottom for stuffing as before. Do not trim the excess fringe.

🔟 Stuff the pillow cover with the polyester fiberfill. Slip-stitch the opening closed. Machine stitch the unstitched section of the fringe trim in place along the lower edge of the pillow, turning under ¼" at the end and trimming the excess.

Materials

**1 Vintage Workshop
Click-n-Craft Cotton
Poplin Fabric Sheet**

∾

**2 rectangles,
6½" x 5½",
of cotton fabric for
pillow front and back**

∾

½ yard of ribbon

∾

**3¾" x 2¾" piece of
paper-backed iron-on
adhesive**

∾

Polyester fiberfill

∾

Thread to match fabric

∾

**Embroidery floss
(optional, for decorative
hand stitching)**

Tools

Clear grid ruler

∾

**Embroidery needle
(optional, for decorative
hand stitching)**

∾

Hand-sewing needle

∾

Iron and ironing board

∾

Pins

∾

**Rotary cutter and
cutting mat**

∾

Scissors

∾

Sewing machine

Hanging Pillow Greeting

Cutting dimensions include ¼" seam allowances.

❶ From the Click-n-Craft CD-ROM, print the hanging pillow greeting image onto the inkjet fabric sheet, following the manufacturer's instructions. Trim the image just inside the marked lines. Remove the paper backing from the image.

❷ Fuse the paper-backed iron-on adhesive to the image, following the manufacturer's instructions. Remove the paper backing. Fuse the image to the center of one of the 6½" x 5½" fabric rectangles, following the manufacturer's instructions.

❸ Stitch around the edges of the image with a decorative machine stitch, such as a buttonhole stitch, or stitch around the image with two strands of embroidery floss and a hand-buttonhole stitch (see page 30 for making buttonhole stitches by hand).

❹ With right sides together, pin the two fabric rectangles together and stitch around the outer edges, leaving a 3" opening for turning. Clip corners, turn right side out, and press.

❺ Stuff the pillow with the polyester fiberfill. Slip-stitch the opening closed.

❻ Tie a knot in each end of the ribbon about 3" from the end. Hand stitch the knot at each end to the top of the pillow, about 1" in from the side edges. Trim the ribbon tails at angles.

Christmas Magnets

Materials
*for 3 Magnets**

1 sheet of high-quality
inkjet paper, matte finish

∽

1 sheet of patterned paper,
such as scrapbook paper

∽

Flat-backed clear glass
stones, such as picture
pebbles, about 1½" in
diameter

∽

PVA craft glue

∽

Hot glue gun and
glue sticks

∽

Glue stick

∽

3 magnet disks,
⅝" in diameter

*When you print the Christmas
images from the Click-n-Craft
CD-ROM, you'll have enough to
make 21 magnets. If you'd like to
use all 21 images, just make sure
you have enough glass stones and
magnet disks.*

Tools

Foam brush

∽

Pencil

∽

Scissors

❶ From the Click-n-Craft
CD-ROM, print the Christmas
images onto inkjet paper. Cut out
three magnet images.

❷ With the glue stick, glue the
images to a piece of patterned
paper, allowing at least 1" between
the images.

❸ Center a glass stone over an
image and trace around it with a
pencil. Cut out the image just
inside the marked lines with
scissors. Repeat for the other
two images.

A Merry
Christmas to you.

❹ With a foam brush, cover the back surface of the glass stone
with PVA craft glue. Center the glass stone on top of the image
and press firmly to secure it in place. Rub gently to remove any
air bubbles or wrinkles. Allow it to dry completely. Repeat for
the remaining two images.

❺ Attach a magnet disk to the back of each glass stone with a
hot glue gun and glue stick.

Tip
To make the greeting cards
shown here, use Spray Mount to adhere
the two Christmas bonus images included
on the CD-ROM to the front of ready-
made blank greeting cards.

Crafts That Say "I Care"

The *Welcome* *Mat*

Oh, let's leave a basket of flowers today
For the little old lady who lives down our way . . .
We'll make it of paper and line it with ferns
Then hide—and we'll watch her surprise when she turns
And opens her door and looks out to see
Who in the world, it could possibly be!

— Virginia Scott Miner

There are so many ways to say "I'm thinking of you!" Let this creative collection be your guide to spreading cheer in the life of someone special. You'll be inspired to add your own flair to these fun projects.

Stitch a pretty seed packet apron for a new neighbor. Create a personalized guest journal for a friend who is getting married. Offer a handcrafted wine bag as a housewarming gift. Or bake a batch of cookies and present it along with a beautiful recipe box.

Whenever you need a little gift-giving inspiration, reach for this resource. Throughout the year you can surprise friends and family—and even the person who seems to have it all—with a special handmade gift from the heart.

Happy is the house that shelters a friend.

— Ralph Waldo Emerson

Materials for 2 Towels

1 Vintage Workshop
Click-n-Craft Iron-On
Transfer Sheet

∿

2 linen hand towels

Tools

Craft knife and
cutting mat

∿

Iron and ironing board

∿

Metal ruler with a
cork back

Guest Towels

❶ From the Click-n-Craft CD-ROM, print the guest towel images onto the iron-on inkjet transfer sheet, following the manufacturer's instructions. Cut out the images. Carefully remove the paper backing from the images.

❷ Center one image from side to side on a towel, about 3½" up from the lower edge. Press in place, following the manufacturer's instructions. Repeat for the remaining towel.

Materials

1 sheet of high-quality inkjet paper, matte finish

❀

Wire-bound journal, horizontal format, 8" x 6"*

❀

1 sheet of decorative paper, such as scrapbook paper

❀

2 sheets of coordinating solid papers, such as scrapbook paper

❀

Spray Mount Artist's Adhesive

❀

Colored eyelets to fit holes along wire binding (optional)

*So that you can easily remove and replace the cover, choose a journal bound with wire loops that you can pull apart rather than a journal bound with a single spiral of wire.

Tools

Craft knife and cutting mat

❀

Eyelet setting tool and hammer (optional, to install eyelets)

❀

Hole punch to match size of holes along wire binding

❀

Metal ruler with cork back

Guest Book

❶ Remove the front cover from the wire binding. For best results, pull wire binding apart slightly where ends meet.

❷ With Spray Mount, adhere decorative paper to the front of the journal cover, applying slight pressure to secure it in place. Trim away the excess paper with a craft knife.

❸ With a hole punch, punch through the decorative paper covering the holes. If desired, install eyelets at each hole, following the manufacturer's instructions.

❹ From the Click-n-Craft CD-ROM, print the roses image onto inkjet paper. Cut out the image. With Spray Mount, adhere the image to the center of the front cover, applying slight pressure to secure it in place.

❺ From the Click-n-Craft CD-ROM, print the word *Guests* onto a piece of solid-colored paper. Trim around the word with a craft knife, creating a rectangular label. With Spray Mount, adhere the label to a coordinating piece of solid-colored paper. Trim 1/16" from the edge of the first piece of paper to create a narrow border. With Spray Mount, adhere the label to the guest book along the lower edge of the rose image.

❻ Reattach the cover to the journal. For best results, align the cover holes to the wire binding where the ends meet. Gently reposition it into place. Press the wire sections together to close the gap where the ends of the binding meet.

Tip
To make this project even easier, purchase a journal that already has a solid or patterned cover that coordinates with the guest book image.

Recipe Box

Materials

1 sheet of high-quality
inkjet paper, matte finish

∾

Unfinished wood box,
about 5¾" long x
3¾" wide x 3¾" high

∾

Patterned tissue paper

∾

Acrylic craft paint to
coordinate with
tissue paper

∾

Three buttons, about
⅜" in diameter

∾

Three buttons, about
¾" in diameter

∾

Spray Mount
Artist's Adhesive

∾

Craft glue

Tools

Craft knife and
cutting mat

∾

Foam brush

∾

Metal ruler with
cork back

∾

Sandpaper, fine-grit

1 With a foam brush, apply a coat of acrylic paint to the outside of the box. Allow it to dry.

2 With a foam brush, apply a thin coat of craft glue to the lid of the box. Lay the tissue paper over the surface of the lid and smooth out the paper with your fingers to eliminate any wrinkles. Trim away the excess paper with a craft knife. Repeat the process for the sides of the lid and box until the surface is completely covered. Allow it to dry completely.

3 Sand the surface of the box lightly to produce a distressed finish.

4 From the Click-n-Craft CD-ROM, print the two recipe box images onto the inkjet paper. Cut out the images.

5 With Spray Mount, adhere the images to the top of the recipe box, allowing about ¼" between the images.

6 Glue the three small buttons between the two images, spacing them evenly. Glue the three large buttons to the center front of the box, spacing them evenly and placing one on the lid and two on the box.

Materials

1 Vintage Workshop
Click-n-Craft Cotton
Poplin Fabric Sheet

∾

Purchased apron with
divided front pocket

∾

12" x 5" piece of paper-
backed iron-on adhesive

Tools

Iron and ironing board

∾

Metal ruler with
cork back

∾

Rotary cutter and
cutting mat

Seed Packet Apron

1 From the Click-n-Craft CD-ROM, print the three seed packet apron images onto the inkjet fabric sheet, following the manufacturer's instructions. Trim the images to include a ¼" border on all sides. Remove the paper backing from the images.

2 Press the ¼" borders to the backs of the images on all sides. Fuse each of the images to a piece of paper-backed iron-on adhesive, following the manufacturer's instructions. Remove the paper backing.

3 Center the leek image on the front bib of the apron, about 1¾" down from the upper edge. Center a seed packet image on each section of the divided pocket. Fuse the images in place, following the manufacturer's instructions.

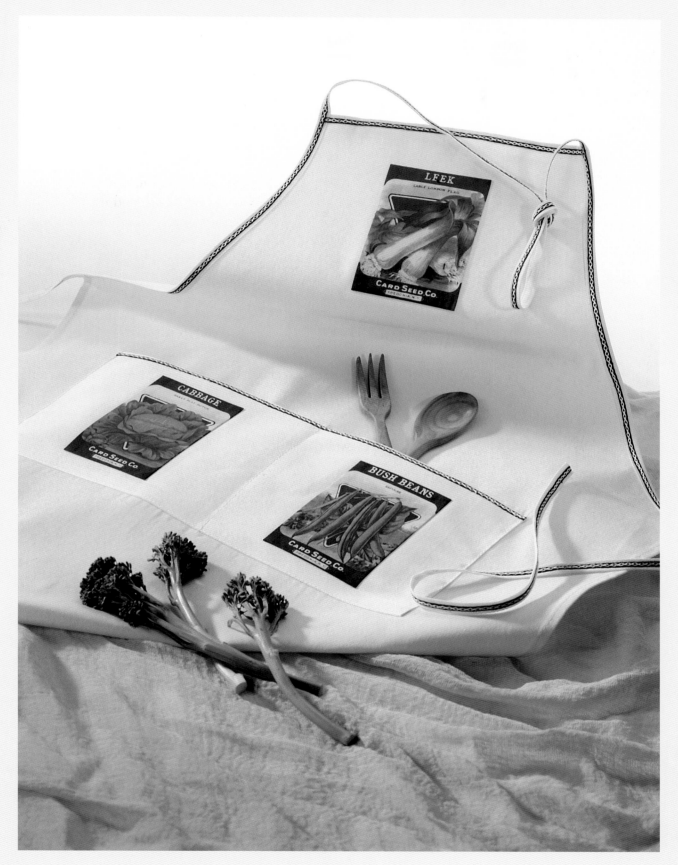

Materials

1 Vintage Workshop Click-n-Craft Cotton Poplin Fabric Sheet

∾

¼ yard of cotton fabric

∾

4½" x 6½" piece of paper-backed iron-on adhesive

∾

1 tasseled curtain tie back

∾

Thread to match fabric

∾

Embroidery floss (optional, for decorative hand stitching)

Tools

Clear grid ruler

∾

Embroidery needle (optional, for decorative hand stitching)

∾

Iron and ironing board

∾

Pins

∾

Rotary cutter and cutting mat

∾

Scissors

∾

Sewing machine

Wine Bag

Cutting dimensions include ¼" seam allowances.

1 Cut a 30" x 6" rectangle from the fabric. Fold the rectangle in half crosswise, wrong sides together.

2 From the Click-n-Craft CD-ROM, print the wine bag image onto the inkjet fabric sheet, following the manufacturer's instructions. Trim the image to include a ¼" border on all sides. Remove the paper backing from the image.

3 Press the ¼" border to the back of the image on all sides. Fuse the image to the piece of paper-backed iron-on adhesive, following the manufacturer's instructions. Remove the paper backing.

4 Position the image on the folded rectangle of fabric, centered from side to side, about 2" up from the fold. Fuse in place, following the manufacturer's instructions.

5 Stitch around the edges of the image with a decorative machine stitch, such as a buttonhole stitch, or stitch around the image with two strands of embroidery floss and a hand-buttonhole stitch (see page 30 for making buttonhole stitches by hand).

6 Fold the rectangle in half crosswise, right sides together, and pin. Stitch along both long edges.

7 Turn the bag right side out and press. Press ¼" to the wrong side around the upper raw edge, then press over ¼" again. Stitch close to the first fold to make a narrow hem.

8 Pinch the bag at the corner, aligning the side seam with

1⅛"

Fig. 1

Hand-tack point in place.

Fig. 2

the fold at the bottom, and press. Measure in 1⅛" from the point and mark with a pin as shown in figure 1. Fold up the corner at the pin mark and press. Remove the pin and hand tack the point in place as shown in figure 2. Repeat on the remaining corner.

❾ Insert a bottle of wine into the bag and tie the bag closed around the neck of the bottle with the tasseled tie back.

Crafts for a Schoolroom with Style

The Classy Classroom

Wisdom outweighs any wealth.

— Sophocles

Show special teachers just how much they are appreciated with these one-of-a-kind gifts! In this chapter, options abound for saying thank you to a favorite teacher in a most original way.

Help a teacher capture memories of the school year with a scrapbook or photo album featuring a handmade cover of the vintage variety. Brighten up a classroom with a decorative terra-cotta plant pot. A personalized lunch bag is both stylish and functional for the busy teacher. Or, create a charming pencil cup for a touch of classroom chic.

Whether you want to thank teachers, tutors, coaches, trainers, or professors, you can surprise them with one of these unique projects that show your gratitude. In return, your thoughtfulness will inspire gratitude toward you.

A teacher affects eternity; he can never tell where his influence stops.

— Henry Brooks Adams

Materials

1 sheet of high-quality inkjet paper, matte finish

∞

Framed chalkboard, about 11" x 17"

∞

1 sheet of decorative paper, such as scrapbook paper

∞

Spray Mount Artist's Adhesive

Tools

Craft knife and cutting mat

∞

Metal ruler with cork back

❶ From the Click-n-Craft CD-ROM, print the chalkboard image onto the inkjet paper. Cut out the image.

❷ With Spray Mount, adhere the image to a sheet of decorative paper, applying slight pressure to secure it in place. Trim ⅛" from the edges of the image to create a narrow border all around.

❸ With Spray Mount, adhere the image to the chalkboard surface, centered from side to side, about ½" below the upper edge of the board. Apply slight pressure to secure it in place.

Materials

1 sheet of high-quality inkjet paper, matte finish

~

Wire-bound journal, 5½" x 4¾"*

~

1 sheet of decorative card stock

~

Spray Mount Artist's Adhesive

~

Eyelets to fit holes along wire binding (optional)

So that you can easily remove and replace the cover, choose a journal bound with wire loops that you can pull apart rather than a journal bound with a single spiral of wire.

Tools

Craft knife and cutting mat

~

Eyelet setting tool and hammer (optional, to install eyelets)

~

Hole punch to match size of holes along wire binding

~

Metal ruler with cork back

School Memories Scrapbook

1 Remove the front cover from the wire binding. For best results, pull the wire binding apart slightly where the ends meet.

2 With Spray Mount, adhere the decorative card stock to the front of the journal cover, applying slight pressure to secure it in place. Trim away the excess paper with a craft knife.

3 With a hole punch, punch through the decorative card stock covering the holes. If desired, install eyelets at each hole, following the manufacturer's instructions.

4 From the Click-n-Craft CD-ROM, print the school memories scrapbook image onto the inkjet paper. Cut out an image just beyond the outer border. With Spray Mount, adhere the image to the center of the front cover, applying slight pressure to secure it in place.

5 Reattach the cover to the journal. For best results, align the cover holes to the wire binding where the ends meet. Gently reposition it in place. Press the wire sections together to close the gap where the ends of the binding meet.

Tip
To make this project even easier, purchase a spiral-bound journal that already has a solid or patterned cover that coordinates with the image.

Materials

1 sheet of high-quality
inkjet paper, matte finish

∾

Terra-cotta pot, about
4" tall and 4½" in diameter
across the top, with a
1¼" rim around the top

∾

Spray Mount
Artist's Adhesive

∾

½ yard of cream ribbon,
about ⅞" wide

∾

½ yard of black ribbon,
about ⅜" wide

∾

⅜ yard of black-and-cream
checked ribbon,
about 1" wide

∾

4" x 3" piece of thin
cardboard

∾

12" length of white
cotton string

∾

Craft glue

Tools

1⁄16" hole punch

∾

Craft knife and
cutting mat

∾

Metal ruler with
cork back

∾

Old paintbrush

∾

Scissors

Terra-Cotta Pot and Tag

❶ From the Click-n-Craft CD-ROM, print the tag image onto inkjet paper. Cut out an image.

❷ With Spray Mount, adhere the image to the cardboard, applying slight pressure to secure it in place. Trim the cardboard even with the edges of the image.

❸ Punch a hole in the upper left corner of the image. Fold the cotton string in half and insert the loop end into the hole from the front of the card. Feed the string tails through the loop and pull snug. Tie the ends in a knot and trim the excess string to complete the tag.

❹ Apply craft glue to the wrong side of the cream ribbon with an old paintbrush and secure the ribbon to the rim of the pot, overlapping the ends by ½" and trimming any excess. Repeat for the black ribbon, centering the black ribbon over the cream ribbon.

❺ Tie the checked ribbon into a bow and glue it to the front of the pot. Trim the ribbon tails at an angle. Allow the glue to dry.

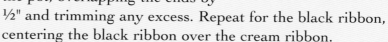
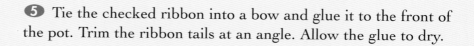

120

Materials

1 Vintage Workshop
Click-n-Craft Cotton
Poplin Fabric Sheet

∾

2 pieces of cotton fabric,
each 11" x 14", for the bag

∾

2 pieces of fusible
interfacing, each 11" x 14"

∾

1 package (3 yards) of
½"-wide, folded bias tape

∾

Thread to match fabric

∾

Contrasting thread for
decorative machine
stitching or embroidery
floss for decorative
hand stitching

∾

4¾" x 7" piece of paper-
backed iron-on adhesive

Tools

Clear grid ruler

∾

Iron and ironing board

∾

Pencil

∾

Rotary cutter and
cutting mat

∾

Scissors

Teacher's Lunch Bag

Cutting dimensions include ¼" seam allowances.

1 From the Click-n-Craft CD-ROM, print the teacher's lunch bag image onto the inkjet fabric sheet, following the manufacturer's instructions. Cut out the image. Remove the paper backing.

2 Press the excess fabric outside the black border to the wrong side along all edges of the image. Fuse the image to the paper-backed iron-on adhesive, following the manufacturer's instructions. Set it aside.

3 Fuse the interfacing to the wrong sides of both fabric pieces, following the manufacturer's instructions.

4 Remove the paper backing from the back of the image. Position one of the fabric rectangles vertically and center the image on the fabric from side to side, about 4" down from the upper edge. Fuse it in place, following the manufacturer's instructions.

5 Stitch around the edges of the image with a decorative machine stitch, such as a buttonhole stitch, or stitch around the image with two strands of embroidery floss and a hand-buttonhole stitch (see page 30 for making buttonhole stitches by hand).

6 With right sides together, pin the bag front and back together. Stitch around the side and bottom edges. Press the seams open.

7 With right sides together, pinch one side seam down to meet the bottom seam, lining them up one on top of another. Secure with a pin. Measure in 1¾" from the corner point and draw a line. Stitch on this line. Trim ¼" away from this stitching. Repeat for the other corner. Turn the bag right side out.

1¾"

Tip

To help the bag
hold its shape at the bottom,
cut a piece of plastic canvas
that measures $3\frac{1}{2}$" x $6\frac{1}{2}$"
and insert it into the
bottom of the bag.

8 Fold the bias tape over the upper edge of the bag
and apply according to the manufacturer's instructions,
turning under the raw edges at the ends.

9 Press a crease at each side of the bag, from the bottom
corner up to the top edge of the bag.

Pencil Cup

Materials

1 sheet of high-quality
inkjet paper, matte finish

Round papier-mâché box,
about 4" tall and 3¾"
in diameter

12" x 12" sheets of
decorative paper,
such as scrapbook paper
(1 sheet each of jade stripe
and burlap print)

Spray Mount
Artist's Adhesive

Tools

Craft knife and
cutting mat

Metal ruler with
cork back

1 Cut a 4½" x 12" piece of jade striped paper. With Spray Mount, adhere the paper to the outside surface of the box, aligning the paper with the lower edge of the box and folding ½" to the inside.

2 Cut a 3¾" x 12" piece from the burlap print paper. With Spray Mount, adhere the paper to the inside of the box.

3 From the Click-n-Craft CD-ROM, print the pencil cup image onto the inkjet paper. Cut out an image. With Spray Mount, adhere the image to a piece of burlap print paper. Trim ⅛" beyond the edges of the image to create a narrow border.

4 With Spray Mount, adhere the image to the center front of the pencil cup.

Resource Directory

~

Check with these manufacturers for a supplier near you.

THE VINTAGE WORKSHOP
www.thevintageworkshop.com
Click-n-Craft CD-ROMs,
inkjet fabric sheets, iron-on transfers,
specialty papers, quilting fabric,
and downloadable art collections

KRYLON
www.krylon.com
Metal primer and enamel paint

PAPER SOURCE
www.paper-source.com
Photo corners

JUDIKINS
www.judikins.com
Picture pebbles

3M
1-866-746-2524
Spray Mount artist's adhesive

UHU
1-800-341-4674
Craft glue stick

PAPER REFLECTIONS BY
DMD INDUSTRIES
www.dmdind.com
Scrapbooks and journals

MAKING MEMORIES
www.makingmemories.com
Miscellaneous papers
K&COMPANY
www.kandcompany.com
Miscellaneous papers

PRYM DRITZ
www.dritz.com
Colored eyelets and tools

K-MART
Tissue box form from
the Martha Stewart Collection

DURWIN RICE
www.durwinrice.com
Glass paperweight

DAN RIVER INC.
www.danriver.com
Fabrics

BAGWORKS
www.bagworks.com
Purchased totes, aprons,
and growth chart

THE WARM COMPANY
www.warmcompany.com
Steam-A-Seam

About the Author

Amy Barickman, founder, owner, and creative director of The Vintage Workshop, grew up in the retail crafting business. She started her own publishing company, Indygo Junction, in 1990 and has since represented the talents of more than 25 designers and leading artists in the craft industry. In her latest venture, The Vintage Workshop, Amy has brought together a new group of talented designers whose projects take crafters to an all-new level of experience. The Click-n-Craft series is a unique program that combines vintage imagery and design work on a CD-ROM, allowing crafters to print high-resolution images with their inkjet printers.

New and Bestselling Titles from

Martingale & Company

America's Best-Loved Craft & Hobby Books®
America's Best-Loved Knitting Books®

That Patchwork Place®

America's Best-Loved Quilt Books®

NEW RELEASES
300 Paper-Pieced Quilt Blocks
American Doll Quilts
Classic Crocheted Vests
Dazzling Knits
Follow-the-Line Quilting Designs
Growing Up with Quilts
Hooked on Triangles
Knitting with Hand-Dyed Yarns
Lavish Lace
Layer by Layer
Lickety-Split Quilts
Magic of Quiltmaking, The
More Nickel Quilts
More Reversible Quilts
No-Sweat Flannel Quilts
One-of-a-Kind Quilt Labels
Patchwork Showcase
Pieced to Fit
Pillow Party!
Pursenalities
Quilter's Bounty
Quilting with My Sister
Seasonal Quilts Using Quick Bias
Two-Block Appliqué Quilts
Ultimate Knitted Tee, The
Vintage Workshop, The
WOW! Wool-on-Wool Folk Art Quilts

APPLIQUÉ
Appliquilt in the Cabin
Blossoms in Winter
Garden Party
Shadow Appliqué
Stitch and Split Appliqué
Sunbonnet Sue All through the Year

Our books are available at bookstores and your favorite craft, fabric, and yarn retailers. If you don't see the title you're looking for, visit us at **www.martingale-pub.com** or contact us at:

1-800-426-3126

International: 1-425-483-3313
Fax: 1-425-486-7596
Email: info@martingale-pub.com

6/04

HOLIDAY QUILTS & CRAFTS
Christmas Cats and Dogs
Christmas Delights
Hocus Pocus!
Make Room for Christmas Quilts
Welcome to the North Pole

LEARNING TO QUILT
101 Fabulous Rotary-Cut Quilts
Happy Endings, Revised Edition
Loving Stitches, Revised Edition
More Fat Quarter Quilts
Quilter's Quick Reference Guide, The
Sensational Settings, Revised Edition
Simple Joys of Quilting, The
Your First Quilt Book (or it should be!)

PAPER PIECING
40 Bright and Bold Paper-Pieced Blocks
50 Fabulous Paper-Pieced Stars
Down in the Valley
Easy Machine Paper Piecing
For the Birds
Papers for Foundation Piecing
Quilter's Ark, A
Show Me How to Paper Piece
Traditional Quilts to Paper Piece

QUILTS FOR BABIES & CHILDREN
Easy Paper-Pieced Baby Quilts
Easy Paper-Pieced Miniatures
Even More Quilts for Baby
More Quilts for Baby
Quilts for Baby
Sweet and Simple Baby Quilts

ROTARY CUTTING/SPEED PIECING
365 Quilt Blocks a Year Perpetual Calendar
1000 Great Quilt Blocks
Burgoyne Surrounded
Clever Quarters
Clever Quilts Encore
Endless Stars
Once More around the Block
Pairing Up
Stack a New Deck
Star-Studded Quilts
Strips and Strings
Triangle-Free Quilts

SCRAP QUILTS
Easy Stash Quilts
Nickel Quilts
Rich Traditions
Scrap Frenzy
Successful Scrap Quilts

TOPICS IN QUILTMAKING
Asian Elegance
Batiks and Beyond
Bed and Breakfast Quilts
Coffee-Time Quilts
Dutch Treat
English Cottage Quilts
Fast-Forward Your Quilting
Machine-Embroidered Quilts
Mad about Plaid!
Romantic Quilts
Simple Blessings

CRAFTS
20 Decorated Baskets
Beaded Elegance
Blissful Bath, The
Collage Cards
Creating with Paint
Holidays at Home
Pretty and Posh
Purely Primitive
Stamp in Color
Trashformations
Warm Up to Wool
Year of Cats...in Hats!, A

KNITTING & CROCHET
365 Knitting Stitches a Year Perpetual Calendar
Beyond Wool
Classic Knitted Vests
Crocheted Aran Sweaters
Crocheted Lace
Crocheted Socks!
Garden Stroll, A
Knit it Now!
Knits for Children and Their Teddies
Knits from the Heart
Knitted Throws and More
Knitter's Template, A
Little Box of Scarves, The
Little Box of Sweaters, The
Style at Large
Today's Crochet
Too Cute! Cotton Knits for Toddlers